Tara Hu...

still
perfectly
I'Mperfect

more remarkable stories of
ordinary women overcoming
extraordinary circumstances

Still Perfectly I'Mperfect
more remarkable stories of ordinary women overcoming extraordinary circumstances
Two Chicks & A Dream Publishing, LLC

Published by Two Chicks & A Dream Publishing, LLC, O'Fallon, MO
Copyright ©2024
All rights reserved.

No part of this publication may be reproduced, stored in a retrieval system, or transmitted in any form or by any means, electronic, mechanical, photocopying, recording, scanning, or otherwise, except as permitted under Section 107 or 108 of the 1976 United States Copyright Act, without the prior written permission of the Publisher. Requests to the Publisher for permission should be addressed to nina@dynamicshiftconsulting.com, please put Perfectly I'Mperfect in the subject line.

Limit of Liability/Disclaimer of Warranty: While the publisher and author have used their best efforts in preparing this book, they make no representations or warranties with respect to the accuracy or completeness of the contents of this book and specifically disclaim any implied warranties of merchantability or fitness for a particular purpose. No warranty may be created or extended by sales representatives or written sales materials. The advice and strategies contained herein may not be suitable for your situation. You should consult with a professional where appropriate. Neither the publisher nor author shall be liable for any loss of profit or any other commercial damages, including but not limited to special, incidental, consequential, or other damages.

All contributing authors to this anthology have submitted their chapters to an editing process, and have accepted the recommendations of the editors at their own discretion. All authors have approved their chapters prior to publication.

Cover, Interior Design, and Project Management:
　Davis Creative Publishing, DavisCreativePublishing.com

Writing Coach and Editor: L. Carol Scott

Compilation by Tara Hurst and Nina DeAngelo

Library of Congress Cataloging-in-Publication Data
(Provided by Cassidy Cataloguing Services, Inc.)
　Names: Hurst, Tara Lipe, compiler. | DeAngelo, Nina, compiler.
　Title: Still perfectly I'Mperfect : more remarkable stories of ordinary women overcoming extraordinary circumstances / compiled by Tara Hurst & Nina DeAngelo.
　Other titles: Still perfectly imperfect
　Description: O'Fallon, MO : Two Chicks & A Dream Publishing, LLC, [2024] | Includes bibliographical references.
　Identifiers: ISBN: 979-8-9889477-3-8 (paperback) | 979-8-9889477-4-5 (hardback) | 979-8-9889477-5-2 (ebook) | LCCN: 2024903537
　Subjects: LCSH: Self-esteem in women. | Imperfection--Psychological aspects. | Motivation (Psychology) | Resilience (Personality trait) | Self-talk. | Life change events--Psychological aspects. | Courage. | LCGFT: Self-help publications. | BISAC: SELF HELP / Motivational & Inspirational. | BODY, MIND & SPIRIT / Inspiration & Personal Growth. | SELF HELP / Personal Growth/Success.
　Classification: LCC: BF697.5.S46 S75 2024 | DDC: 158.1--dc23

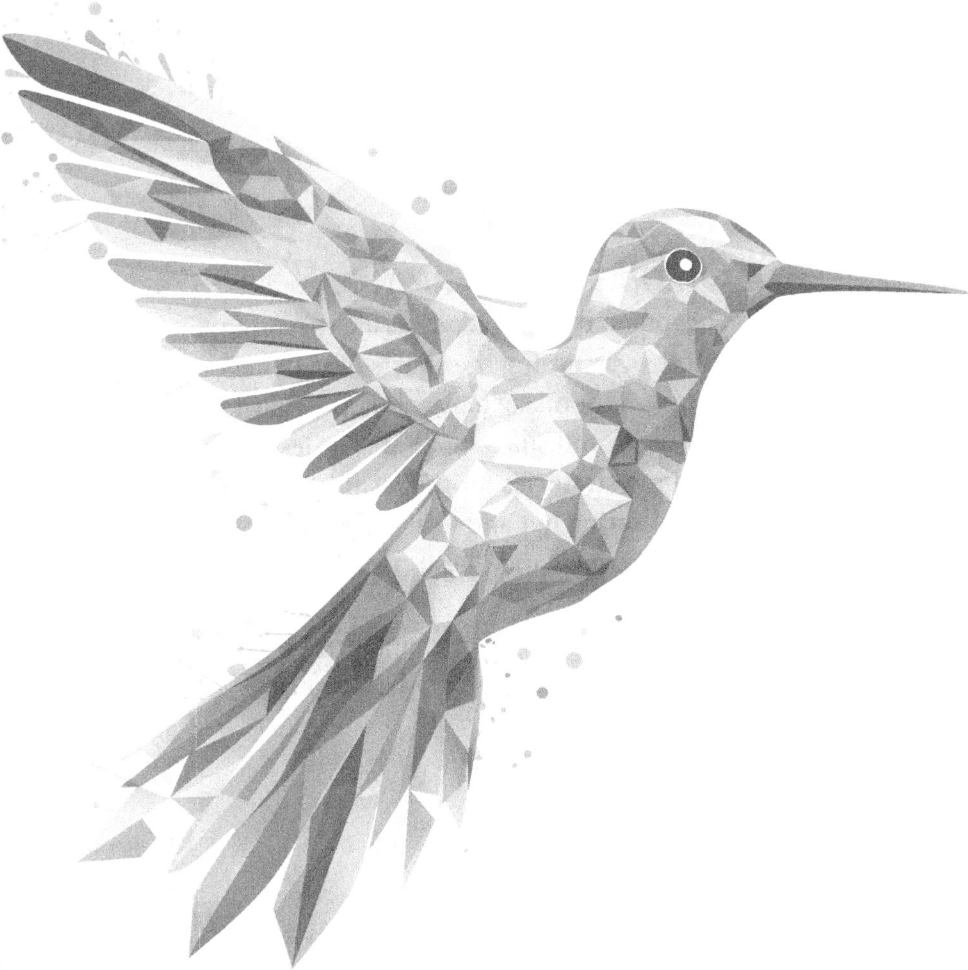

TRIGGER WARNING:
Several chapters in this book describe the authors' experiences overcoming the effects of violence—including childhood sexual assault and marital abuse, self-harm and suicide—as well as less-than-positive coping strategies for the resulting trauma, such as sexual acting out and overuse of alcohol and both prescribed and illegal street drugs.

We have identified these chapters with a DAISY ❀ to empower reader's choice.

Table of Contents

Stacey O'Byrne | Foreword ix
Tara Hurst | Journey From Fear to Faith 1
Nina DeAngelo | Surviving a Narcissist 8
Kathy Goughenour | Laughing All the Way 14
Kelly Godar | Beyond the Curse 20
Pam Kueker | Grief Bakes a Cake 25
Jenn Cobbel | Bottom of the Barrel 31
Katie Gearin | No Longer Silent: The Journey to Finding My Voice . 37
Dr. Jennifer Capler | Reflections 44
Heather Calvin | I Am Not a Piece of Sh*t 50
Jennifer Whitehead | Redefining Success 56
Aliesha Pollino | Not Stuck, Not Stoppin'! 62
Amy Jones | Borderline Angel ✿ 69
Dr. Kristin Gaines Porlier | The Voice Inside 75
April Imming | My Happily Ever After 82
Nancy Ortinau | Seeds of Resilience:
   Cultivating Healing and Growth 89
Michelle Huelsman | A Farewell's Echo 95
Abiegayle Winingar | Where Is My Respect?! 102
Helen Black | "I Am Here for You," He Said ✿ 108
Jerileigh Farrell | To Be Continued ✿ 115
April Keubler | From Surviving to Thriving 121
Marcia Rodriguez | Knock, Knock. Who's There? 128

Karyn Williams | The One That Got Away ✿ 135

Kerri Landis | The Worst Year of My Life 141

Jan Kraus | My Life As a Statistic 147

Kim Skief | Give Yourself Grace 155

Stella Webb | Holy and Healing ✿ 161

Laura LaMarca | I Am Sick of Being Sick. 167

Loryl Breitenbach | Going Out on a Limb Is the Path 173

Eliza Poe | Desperately Seeking Myself. 179

Justine Wilson | Just One More Day. 186

Tammy Egelhoff | Toto, We Aren't in Kansas Anymore!. 193

Andrea Allen | Awakenings 198

Derlene Hirtz | Becoming The Woman in The Mirror 205

Sheila Riggs | Becoming My Own Advocate. 211

Ann Langston | From Shouting and Silence to Saving the Kids . . . 217

Layla Evans | Who Am I? ✿ 223

Kay Pierson | Home ✿ 229

Lori Stock | Embrace the Suck 236

Jessica Beeson | Who Makes the D*mn Rules, Anyway? 242

Dr. L. Carol Scott | Childhood Replayed. 248

Cathy Davis | The Bird's the Word 255

Stacey O'Byrne

Foreword

Let's get real here and cut right to the chase. *STILL Perfectly I'Mperfect* is your wake-up call to the raw, unfiltered reality of what it means to navigate all the trials and tribulations life's path presents to us. It is more than just another book; it's a battle cry, a declaration from forty women who have been through the wringer and come out on the other side armed with stories that will touch your heart, relate to your journey, and, in some cases, rock you to your core. These aren't just feel-good, fluffy stories. They are raw, real, and riveting journeys of women who have stared down the barrel of defeat and refused to blink an eye. They're not just surviving; they're thriving and doing it their way—flaws and all.

In working with tens of thousands of business owners, entrepreneurs, and sales professionals as a speaker, trainer, mentor, and success strategist, the first step to true empowerment is owning your story, the mess, the setbacks, the comebacks, the drama, the trauma and all the imperfect moments in between. I've seen firsthand how embracing your true self, imperfections included, can catapult you to new heights. This book is a powerhouse of those truths. Each story packs a punch, showing that success is far from avoiding the pitfalls of life and more about how you climb out, dust off, and use the lessons learned to forge a path forward. This book embodies that philosophy. Each author has transformed their darkest hours into their brightest achievements, providing you with a front-row seat to the kind of resilience and determination that refuses to accept defeat.

These authors aren't just sharing stories; they're handing you the playbook on how to navigate challenges with tenacity and nerve. They've faced down everything from personal tragedies and health crises to professional and societal barriers that many wouldn't dare to tackle. Yet, here they stand, not just standing but stepping boldly into their power. These forty women come from diverse backgrounds, and their challenges are as unique as their fingerprints. Yet, each story converges on a common theme: embracing imperfections not just as a part of life but as the very essence of life.

STILL Perfectly I'Mperfect tears down the facades and helps you realize life and living empowered is a choice and is about owning every part of your journey: the good, the bad, the ugly, and especially the imperfect. It exposes the truth that success is messy, can have its tough moments, and yes, it's feedback, which some label as a failure. Here's the reality: those failures are not the opposite of success; they are part of the journey to success. It's about understanding that your imperfections are far from quirks or limitations; they are your strengths mislabeled by society's projections.

Each author's chapter peels back the layers of pretense to reveal the core of true empowerment and authenticity. It shows you why the path to victory isn't paved with constant wins but with continuous learning, adjusting, and persevering.

Each woman in this collaborative collection does more than share her journey. Each chapter is a masterclass in overcoming obstacles, struggling, grasping for survival, and victory. These women don't hold back. They reveal their fears, pains, and triumphs with a transparency that is both vulnerable and powerful. They teach us that the greatest battles we face will not define us; rather, they create us, and how we handle these battles will absolutely define us.

Buckle up and prepare to be inspired by a journey of tenacity that redefines what it means to be vulnerable and victorious at the same time. You'll read about women who have reshaped their destinies through sheer will and unwavering determination. You'll learn about the transformative power of hitting rock bottom and finding there's nowhere to go but up. And you'll see that sometimes, the only way out is through—through the pain, through the fear, and through the doubt.

They also challenge you to reflect on your own life. It's an invitation to look at your imperfections and see them for what they really are—not barriers, but invitations to rise above and become more than you ever thought possible. It's a call to look at the scars of your past and see them as badges of honor, symbols of what you have endured and overcome. This isn't just a book; it's a movement. It's a call to action for anyone who's ever felt knocked down by life to stand up and push back with all the might of a woman who knows her worth and refuses to be defined by her circumstances. It's a testament to the strength of the human spirit and a celebration of every woman who has dared to say, "I am perfectly imperfect, and that is my strength."

STILL Perfectly I'Mperfect builds a community. It's a testament to the strength found in unity, in sharing our stories and discovering that we are not alone in our struggles. By turning these pages, you join a tribe of warriors who have transformed their deepest vulnerabilities into their greatest strengths.

Here's to the perfectly imperfect journeys of these remarkable women. Here's to fighting the good fight and emerging not unimpacted or affected but unapologetically victorious. Here's to living a life that's real, not one that's devoid of problems but one that embraces every challenge as a stepping stone to greater heights.

So buckle up. These stories will take you on a wild ride of emotion, reflection, challenge, and triumph. Prepare to be inspired, to laugh, to cry, to cheer, and most of all, to change. Because after reading *STILL Perfectly I'Mperfect,* you won't just be moved. Like the women in these chapters, you'll be inspired and motivated to move your mountains.

It's time to get out of your way and get on your way so you can finally have your way and design the life you have always known you dream of, desire, and know you deserve.

Let's make shift happen,

Stacey O'Byrne
Pivot Point Advantage
www.pivotpointadvantage.com
staceyobyrne@pivotpointadvantage.com

Tara Hurst

Journey From Fear to Faith

Faith and fear are both invisible … When life begins to spiral uncontrollably around us, we decide which—faith or fear—we will grab and hold tightly in the middle of the storm. More than once, I have found myself inside raging winds and torrential rains that made it almost impossible to see. Lost in the dark, I was bombarded with the debris of mental, emotional, and physical pain, struggling to find the lesson in it all.

I was a typical kid growing up in the 1970s and '80s. Climbing trees, drinking water from a garden hose, roller skating, and riding bikes all over the neighborhood until the streetlights came on. I sat for hours making clover bracelets and headbands in our front yard, only to do it all over again the next day.

Being the youngest and only girl, I could be wearing a dress and have bows in my hair, and still win a neighborhood fight. Wasn't this normal? Didn't everyone learn at a very young age to protect themselves and fight back?

All through school I was the person who others came to for protection, or the one called on when they needed help. I wasn't the cool kid, or the rich kid, or the nerd, or the jock. I was simply the girl who no one seemed to mess with more than once.

I also grew up hearing that I was fat, ugly, worthless, and not good enough. At that time in my life I endured a sexual assault that has played over and over in my head for years. It wasn't just an attack on my body; it felt like an assault on my very worth. It wrapped my heart in thick, suffocating vines of guilt, shame, and anger. Low self-esteem, negative inner chatter, and limiting beliefs became part of me. Those feelings and thought patterns grew stronger and stronger as I grew older. How could I allow others to love me when I didn't even love myself? The truth was not easy, because at times I was very difficult to love.

I grew up, got married, started a family, and thought everything would magically change. In reality, I still lived in fear. Every decision I made, conversation I held, or question I posed or pondered then repeated over and over in my mind. I worried: *What will they think? What will they say? What if this, what if that? What if?* Holy sh*t that was *exhausting*! I wasn't only struggling to love myself; I didn't even trust myself.

Isn't it fascinating how many ways we can hide our traumas from each other and even ourselves? I had stuffed mine deep down inside so that I didn't have to think about it or feel it. I internalized all the hurt and pain and created an outward appearance of confidence and certainty. When emotional storms blew, I was always the calm one, managing the whole situation. But all the while I quietly relived every emotional scene, endlessly questioning myself and my choices. So, at forty years of age, I realized I was punishing myself when I was not responsible for events outside of my control. I woke up to how afraid I was, and I realized fear is a liar.

Have you ever reached such a breaking point? I experienced mine as an instantaneous *knowing* that I was just done—done being ignored and done being disrespected. From one breath to the next, I found myself no longer willing to accept the way things were and had always been. I was finished with buying into the lie of "that's just how they are; they will never change." No longer concerned with others changing, *I* was changing.

I recall walking into my mom's kitchen, defeated, and tears pooling in my eyes. I yearned for her to tell me that life was going to get better. I looked at her and asked, "Is this really as good as it gets?" As good moms have done for generations, she simply hugged me. Knowing she could not fix my internal struggles, she gently showed me how she would love me through my own efforts to mend it.

My body was the biggest it had ever been. I was miserable, depressed, and parenting from the couch, exhausted, inflamed, and in pain. My diagnoses included fibromyalgia, chronic fatigue, restless leg syndrome, and degenerative disc disease. I also suffered from migraines and lived with a knee that began deteriorating after a long-ago injury and continued to after three surgical attempts to fix it. Years of carrying guilt, shame, anger, and self-doubt had taken their toll on my body, as well as my heart and mind. I was punishing my body because I didn't feel worthy of loving or respecting myself. And my body shouted its signals of struggle at the daily neglect.

At last, my growing self-awareness began to transform into self-love. I embraced the realization that I am not only what I eat and drink, I am also who I surround myself with, whose voices I allow into my life. I am blessed with compassionate, patient, and loving parents, an encouraging husband, and joy-inducing, lifelong friends. What if, beyond these nurturing loved ones, I began nurturing myself, controlling the story in my head, and allowing faith to kick fear right in the teeth?

I knew this new approach to life wasn't going to be easy and would require patience and grace. At this point, I simply chose a new version of *hard*. My growth required some pruning, much like a flowering bush must be cut back to flourish. I cut away toxic relationships, negative thought patterns, and sabotaging behaviors, allowing new blooms: people who uplifted me and supported me in my growth.

On my own, I released one hundred pounds of self-doubt, negative self-talk, low self-esteem, worthlessness, and feelings of not being enough. I claimed victory in a war I had been struggling to win since that little girl made clover necklaces in my front yard. The fallout from that battle was one hundred pounds of heavy armor. Over fifteen months, I finally set down that armor, which I had willingly worn to protect me from every storm I faced.

And then I realized the heart of the matter: I didn't need to be fixed, because I wasn't broken. Those fifteen months forever changed the trajectory of my life.

Step one was an honest look at what I could change in my current lifestyle. I wasn't active, so I planned to walk a few times a week: first to the mailbox, then to the stop sign, then hiking the hills around my home. It took me six months to finally conquer those hills. I looked objectively at what I ate and drank daily and made simple adjustments like replacing pasta with zucchini, or ordering broccoli in place of french fries, drinking water instead of diet soda, and choosing lean proteins in place of fast food. Sugar? Kicked it. Boundaries? Honored them. Goals? Made them. I began to realize that every moment, I was only one decision away from a completely different life.

With each passing day, month, and year, I became physically stronger, although I still wore the tattered rags of my mental and emotional wounds like a blue ribbon, almost a badge of honor. Strength training two or three days per week, hiking three times per week, and high-intensity interval training (HIIT) three times per week, I pushed my body to the limit, adding activities like Tough Mudders on the weekends.

Then it happened. I injured my knee yet again and was faced with this choice: wear a heavy metal brace except when sleeping or have a total knee replacement. This setback returned me to my familiar old pattern of self-doubt and overthinking. Again, I felt unworthy of wellness, and I stopped honoring the commitment I had made to a new life, gaining back twenty-five pounds.

This time, I also learned the lesson that one cannot out-train a poor diet. No amount of gym time could balance out the fat and sugar I was consuming. I had worked so hard to lose weight and wondered why I was now losing ground.

In fact, I knew what to do but wasn't doing it. So once again, I took a leap of faith and enrolled in a nutrition program that included working with a coach. I now realize how pivotal this decision was. For the first time, I allowed someone to tell me how to do something *their way*, and I actually listened and trusted the process, without letting fear play that continuous loop of self-doubt in my head.

In 2020 another kind of storm hit, and my husband lost both of his jobs to the pandemic quarantines. Living paycheck to paycheck with two kids in college and not qualifying for any type of government relief was a whole new level of frightening. We needed to get creative or lose our home, our cars, and the life we had created.

Choice is a beautiful thing. I could easily have allowed the stress to overwhelm me, to return me to those negative thought patterns that I carried throughout childhood. Instead, I prepared for battle; this time I wasn't fighting alone. Though I often felt it was me against the world, God had been walking beside me the entire time. From the neighborhood Methodist church I attended on my own as a child, to the Baptist church I attended with my best friend throughout grade school, to the Presbyterian church where I worked when we lived in Nashville, to the nondenominational church I now attend on a regular basis, God has been there right beside me.

When I finally understood this truth, faith completely overtook fear.

In April of that year, I jumped feetfirst into something new, coaching others to greater health. Rather than think the opportunity to death, this time I had faith in my success. Three months later, in another leap of faith, my husband and I bought a building, and we opened a record store three months after that. Clearly, God had a hand in this story with little miracles like the owner offering to finance our loan, and our friends and family enabling us to open in just nine weeks.

What happened next almost took me down. I have never in my life experienced such darkness in a storm. In January of 2022 I had a total knee replacement, and it appeared my body was rejecting the hardware from the procedure. Not only was I in excruciating daily pain and unable to walk unassisted without fear of falling, but all the soft tissue around my knee was also swollen and inflamed. I was going backward again, after all my progress.

Thank God for my sweet mama who was right by my side, because at times I felt bewildered and ready to give up. My independence was gone, and I had lost the version of me that I'd spent ten years building. Yet my entire life is becoming a series of lessons, and I am learning to honor who I am and where I am going.

At each downturn, I always have a choice: continue to sit in my sh*t and remain focused on my limitations, or focus on what I *can* do and go from there. Once I turned my fear into faith, I realized that faith doesn't prevent life's storms but empowers me to move through them, because I was made for more.

Tara Hurst is an empowerment and transformation coach who specializes in mindfulness and inner chatter and how they affect health and fitness, energy and spirituality, advancement in business, and relationships of all types. Tara is a neuro-linguistic programming (NLP) master coach and trainer, a business mentor, public speaker, and #1 International Bestselling author. After releasing one hundred pounds and beginning a personal healing journey, Tara began coaching others and empowering their transformations with daily habits to improve their emotional, mental, spiritual, and physical well-being. Tara works individually with clients to motivate, encourage, and support them, enabling them to build self-confidence, set new goals, and seek growth in every aspect of their lives.

Nina DeAngelo

Surviving a Narcissist

It was 4:00 p.m. and I had not gotten my daily phone call from him. This routine was set for the "good days." I picked up my phone, unable to swallow as I dialed his phone number, hoping and praying he would answer. The line rang and rang as I waited with a knot in the pit of my stomach and the feeling that I might vomit. When the phone connected to his voicemail, I knew.

We met in the military, when we were both stationed in Panama, South America. He was a tall, blond, sparkling blue-eyed, tanned Adonis. His smile across the commissary aisle took my breath away and captured my heart all in one instant. I was mesmerized that quickly. I had six weeks left in Panama and he was just arriving. I had already spent a good part of four years there, and I was lonely. I'd just been broken eight months earlier by a relationship that had taken my whole heart and soul … and my goodness, this commissary babe was a sight for sore eyes.

He followed me out of the commissary with his cart full of groceries and seemed to be watching me. I knew he was behind me, as I was keeping my eye on him as well. Once we exited the building, I went to my car and he went to his, on the *opposite* side of the parking lot! I was like, *What the what?* I kept an eye on him as he loaded his car up. Once he was done, I looked right at him, threw my arms and hands up, and gave him the "what's up" movement. He looked at me, put his head down, smiled, and then walked over.

From that point, we courted briefly, and this is where the red flags started to show. But I was in a place in my life when I did not want to see or acknowledge them. He was super charismatic. He was good looking, funny, intelligent ... and would pick fights with me just so we could "make up." Then he'd shower me with gifts and praise.

I remember distinctly this one fight we had: he was being a complete jack*ss, and I'd decided enough was enough. I didn't have much time left in Panama, and I didn't have to put up with his sh*t. We were at his barracks, and I didn't want to be around him anymore, so I left and started walking back to my place, a good three miles away. I felt the walk would help me clear my head and decide what to do next. You see, joining the military as a young female, I developed a very tough skin, and I believed if I could make it in the military, I could make it anywhere. I had self-worth, self-trust, and I believed in me.

I was about a half mile away from his barracks when he pulled up next to me and apologized for being an a**hole. Hearing an apology from a man was something I was not used to. It struck me as genuine. I believed that he understood his behavior to be less than desirable and wanted to make things right. So, like any smitten young lady, I accepted his apology, hopped into the car, and off we went to "make up."

"Don" and I got married a week or so after I left Panama. He traveled to Fort Carson on leave, and we had a courthouse wedding. Remember: this is just a few short weeks after we met for the first time. Eighteen months later, he followed me to Colorado on his new duty assignment, and we began living as a couple.

Our marriage was full of ups and downs. We were two young adults, each figuring out life for ourselves and not ready to consider another whole person in our decisions and lifestyle choices. However, we were determined to make this relationship work regardless of our short time together and not truly knowing each other.

After we were together in Colorado, Don's health took a turn. He was in constant pain and wasn't sleeping well due to this pain, which made it difficult to get out of bed in the mornings and be at the base on time.

Don was a firm believer in healing himself. He ate well, he exercised regularly, and he believed with every fiber of his being that he would overcome whatever this misalignment he was currently dealing with was.

Don was eventually diagnosed with fibromyalgia. Back in the mid- to late-1990s, there wasn't a lot of information about this condition or how it should be treated. So the almighty wisdom of military doctors prescribed him a pill to wake up in the morning and a pill to go to sleep at night. I truly believe that is when the downward spiral of our marriage released a red flag too big to ignore.

Don was medically discharged from the military. He was a sixteen-year career soldier: Air Assault, Airborne, a Ranger … and he even went through Green Beret training twice. He had been in the military since he was a teenager and didn't know any other way of life. To now be discharged from the one thing he loved, and to be dependent on the cocktail of medications prescribed by his doctors, was a recipe for disaster.

Don eventually found a job selling for a local car dealer, and with his charisma and charm, he did very well. That sales job landed him another high-paying sales job with an oil and gas tycoon.

But while working for the car dealer, he had developed a taste for drugs and alcohol. When he started working for the oil and gas tycoon, this abuse escalated, as it was a normal way of life for his coworkers. Looking back now, I see Don's use of drugs and alcohol was just another way for him to mask his pain and disappointment in himself.

And then there was the money. When he started this new job working in oil and gas, it was nothing unusual for Don to bring home $30,000 each month. This was a lot of money that neither of us were used to having. And the income led to more problems.

He would eventually escalate his drug use to crack, meth, and heroin. Our marriage became a nightmare. We had two small children to care for, and because Don was making so much money on his own, he wanted me to stay home and care for the house and our children.

About two years into this routine of life, the bad dream became a nightmare. First, Don started coming home late from work. When he *did* get home, he was in one of two states: 1) drunk or high or both, exhausted, and ready for bed, or 2) drunk or high or both, pissed off, and angry at the world. Coming home late eventually became staying out overnight, which then turned into being gone days at a time. I was so confused and so lost. But the financial stability we had was something I was not willing to give up.

Before the extracurricular drug use started, Don had developed a routine. He called me by lunchtime every day to say "hi" and that he was thinking of me. All of that stopped when he went on benders.

And that's when I knew he was not coming home. As the drug abuse escalated, he became more verbally and emotionally abusive and eventually even stole my identity. But I'm not talking about the crime of identity theft. No, I'm talking about making me question who I was as an individual, and my worth and purpose as a wife, as a mother, and as a human on this planet. Those who knew me before this relationship began to say things like, "Nina, you aren't the same strong, independent person we once knew." I didn't believe them. I didn't listen to their warnings, and I kept fighting for my marriage. That fight would eventually end up with

Don doing two stints in rehab, only to come out and be back to his old ways within weeks of recovery.

I was mentally and emotionally exhausted from the constant love bombing and gaslighting that became my everyday norm. I cried to my mother and my sister, wondering what I did to deserve such a sh*t life. I lived in a space of victimhood that did not serve me or my greater purpose and was certainly not productive and stable for my children. Then, one day I faced the toughest decision of my life. My best choice for me and my children was to leave Don to his self-destruction and move away from this relationship. I had to take my kids and leave. Life would not get any better by living in the same condition.

So I left. I made the decision one night to pack my bags and my kids' bags and drive eleven hours from Texas to my mother's house in Missouri. And that is when a life-changing inner journey, the true journey to rediscover me, started.

Leaving was not easy; it was not fun, and it downright sucked and scared me to death. Making a decision that changed the trajectory of my life was the hardest thing I've ever done. And you know what? It was also the most rewarding thing I've ever done. I came to see that I am worthy of an amazing life and have a purpose here on this planet. I loved myself enough to pull up my bootstraps and get the h*ll out of what was not serving me.

Nina DeAngelo is a highly skilled Neuro-Linguistics Programming (NLP) master coach and trainer, and an empowerment speaker. With years of experience, Nina has honed her expertise in NLP to empower individuals and teams to reach their full potential. Through her dynamic coaching and training sessions, she has helped hundreds of individuals unlock their inner strengths, overcome obstacles, and achieve personal and professional success. As an engaging and inspiring speaker, Nina captivates audiences with her motivating messages of self-empowerment, resilience, and personal growth. She is known for her warm, friendly approach, which creates a safe and supportive environment for growth and transformation. Aspiring leaders in corporations and nonprofits seek out Nina as a coach and teacher for both personal and professional development. As her passion unlocks their true potential, they find greater purpose and fulfillment in their lives. Nina's zeal for helping others shines in every interaction and makes her a sought-after coach, trainer, and speaker in the field of personal and professional development as she guides individuals to unlock their true potential and live a life of purpose and fulfillment.

Kathy Goughenour

Laughing All the Way

Crying in your cubicle at work isn't a good career move. But that's what I did when my boss told me I would never again get promoted after almost twenty years with "the phone company."

The first time I asked him "Why am I not getting promoted?" he replied, "You lack a master's degree." Off to night school I trotted, determined to acquire that master's degree in Business Administration. Approaching it with my characteristic zeal and determination, I concentrated and graduated in two years, summa cum laude, at the spry young age of forty.

My boss congratulated me on that achievement. Then awarded the next promotion to a twenty-something who hadn't even attained a bachelor's degree.

After reading the announcement, I marched into his office and asked, "Why didn't I get that promotion?" He gruffly asked, "Do you want to know the truth?" "Yes!" I almost screamed. "Of course I want to know the truth. I wanted to know the truth two years ago when you told me I needed a master's degree."

He smirked at me and said, "You laugh and smile too much. And until you change that, you'll never get promoted again at this company."

Shocked, I could barely move. Tears flooded my eyes, and I scurried out of his office before the drops poured and formed a puddle at my feet.

Victimhood doesn't look good on anyone and certainly not on me. That's one of many reasons I'd been working with a psychologist for the previous decade. I'd struggled to get past the childhood trauma from my father being killed by a drunk driver when I was only eight years old. That accident left me with a mother who didn't want me, who told me about her many failed attempts to abort me, who pretended I didn't exist: ignoring holidays, birthdays and routine motherly acts of kindness like meals and clothing. I survived my childhood, learned to thrive as an adult, and I surely wasn't going to let this b*tthead boss get me down.

After my crying jag in my tiny cubicle, I pulled my big-girl panties up—metaphorically, of course—and dug into my library of self-help books. I landed on one called *Wishcraft* by Barbara Sher. In it she teaches how to identify what you want and how to go for it. I put her recommendations into action.

Within six months of hearing I'd "never be promoted again," I walked into the boss man's office, but this time with a smile on my face—you know, the smile that he claimed appeared too frequently—and handed him my resignation. "You can't quit," he blustered, after scanning the letter.

"Oh, I know I *can* quit. And a resignation letter is the official way to do it," I replied coolly.

Sneeringly, he said, "No, I mean you can't quit because you'll never earn this kind of money anywhere else. You're forty years old. No one will hire you for the salary you're earning here."

"I'll not only replace that income, I'll double it!" I shouted with conviction. I have no idea where "double it" came from, but those words were out of my mouth before they registered in my brain.

Two weeks later, unemployed and with my "I quit" confidence now lost, I began experiencing post-traumatic stress symptoms: nerves, anxiety, nightmares, and night sweats. My recurring nightmare was that I had quit "wrong" and they forced me to return to my job. I'd wake up from that dream terrified … and then thankful that it was only a dream.

Had I made a mistake quitting? Doubts started to creep in. Every person I knew, all my work colleagues, my family, and my friends, had tried to talk me out of quitting. They said, "You're forty! You only have fifteen more years to retirement. Hang in there."

Back to the self-help books I went, and learned how to nurture myself. What a concept! Care for myself as I would care for anyone I love. The nightmares stopped, my confidence grew, and I knew I was on the right track. At the age of forty, I had another lifetime ahead of me. A lifetime I didn't want to squander watching the office clock slowly tick by for fifteen more years. A lifetime I wanted to live with joy.

During my last few years at my corporate job, I'd applied for a sales position. I was turned down there, too, because I "didn't have what it took to be a salesperson."

But I knew better. So when the opportunity arose to sell for a multi-level marketing (MLM) company and have my own business, I jumped at it. Within six months, I was breaking sales records. Over the next three years, I continued to break records and win every award and trip the company offered. My confidence increased as I learned what it took to sell, and I loved it.

Unfortunately, there was a downside: While I brought in millions for the company, their payout formula provided only $10,000 annually in profit for me. Not nearly what I'd been earning in my corporate job, much less twice as much. My boss's prediction was coming true.

My husband, Tom, had an opportunity to work as a contractor in Halifax, Nova Scotia. All living expenses would be covered, and he invited me to join him for the six months he'd be there. After reviewing my profits with the MLM business (still pitifully low) and weighing the pros and cons of closing that business and moving to Nova Scotia for six months (essentially a six-month vacation), I decided I needed that down time to consider what to do next.

My husband and I spent those six glorious months reconnecting, exploring Nova Scotia, and meeting some of the nicest people in the world. I relaxed, read voraciously, and rejuvenated. This sojourn allowed me to take time for me—time to reflect and consider what I really wanted to do next.

Six months turned into three years, during which I followed Tom's career. After Nova Scotia he was offered a position in Northern California, then a position in Kansas City, Missouri. Each time we moved, I searched the web for real estate agents who'd help us secure a fabulous home.

One of those agents was Mike. His website needed improvement, and I told him so when we talked, giving him some suggestions for improvement. He said, "Put your skills where your mouth is and fix it for me." And I did. Mike liked the work I did and continued using my skills to perform marketing tasks for him. For the first time ever, I worked remotely … from my home in Kansas City, Missouri.

Then, in 2001, the company Tom was working for suddenly closed their doors. Not wanting to go back to a corporate job, I convinced Tom that I could work and support us from a tiny cabin we owned in the middle of a Southern Missouri national forest. I asked Mike if I could keep working for him if I moved there, and he said, "Of course you can, you're a virtual assistant, a VA."

I'd never heard that term, so I researched it and found that a VA was exactly the role I'd been providing for Mike: working remotely as an independent contractor.

As I always did, I dove into this new business with focus and determination. And within three years, I'd developed a six-figure business. Which means I'd *doubled* my corporate salary. Success!

I loved the freedom and flexibility of working for myself from home, and continued to experience success. At the peak of my VA business, I had seventy real estate agents as clients, with a waiting list of fifteen or more at all times.

As one of only a handful of six-figure VAs at the time, my success began to attract women from around the USA and Canada. They contacted me to find out if I could help them start a VA business and achieve similar success. In 2008, I launched my training program for VAs, now called Virtual Expert® Training, and I've never looked back.

Helping women like me to feel fulfilled and validated, and to find the freedom, flexibility, and financial security they desire and deserve makes me smile. And now I laugh all the way to the bank!

Kathy Goughenour is the founder of Virtual Expert® Training, where she teaches professional women how to build their own work-from-anywhere Virtual Expert businesses. Kathy runs her virtual empire from her dream home, which is a tiny cabin in the middle of a Missouri national forest. She can be found sporting a tiara most of the time. And she wears PJs (not gowns). Yes, you got it. PJs and tiaras … because that's the type of kingdom she's ruling. And why not? Kathy knows that when you become a powerful woman, you can make your own rules.

Kelly Godar

Beyond the Curse

I am a miracle. The death of my husband from lung cancer, chronic debilitating headaches that manifested as an aneurysm and dropped me into darkness in a moment, loss of a month of my life, and the challenges of recovery and physical therapy were not experiences I ever imagined for my life. Nor could I have imagined all of this before the age of fifty.

Then came November 24, 2021, Chicago. That evening in a hotel room, I reacted in a way I could not live with any longer. On the "morning after" this distinct episode, the memory of my actions the night before decked me just as that aneurysm had a year before. That was my "drop to my knees" moment.

I was still reeling from life's earlier body blow. Though eight years behind me, the 2013 lung cancer and the death of my husband had turned my life upside down. Watching my spouse fight this terminal disease was the most heartbreaking experience of my life, not only for me, but for his children as well. Eight years before, I hadn't known how I was going to live without him. Just thirty-nine years old, I was living my worst nightmare.

Carl and I had a great marriage, and he was my best friend. Was I being punished for living a happy life? Looking back from that Chicago vantage point of eight years, I could see that just asking myself this question brought the very curse from God I came to believe: I was destined to not live a happy life. That curse seemed to haunt me after Carl died. Only later did I realize I had turned to using alcohol at night to drown my cursed mindset.

Carl and I had worked together in the family's small business before his death, so I found myself tasked with much more responsibility because there was no replacement available for him. Then, in the summer of 2020 I developed terrible headaches that I thought were stress related from the extra workload. At times the pain caused me to step away from my desk. Sometimes I even went home and rested for a bit, but more often I just sat in my vehicle in hopes that the pain would ease.

The headaches interfered so much with my work, I felt compelled to reach out to my physician. I got dizzy and sick to my stomach yet did not have a history of migraines. In fact, I had never experienced any headaches of this intense nature. When pain medication provided no relief, my doctor scheduled an MRI. Unfortunately, the MRI didn't show anything, and I was left to figure out this mystery condition on my own.

With the help of friends, family, and a therapist, my life also moved on in these few years after Carl's death, and I was able to find love again. Life was going well, I was on track to getting my headaches under control (so I thought), I was working out three to four times a week and trying to eat healthier. You know how it goes: a new year is right around the corner, so why not get a jump start on having the best year yet? Then, Christmas Day, my new boyfriend proposed! *Yes!* Finally, 2021 was going to be my year.

The next day I went to the gym feeling energized, happy, and filled with optimism for a momentous year. And so it would be ... but not for the reasons I'd hoped. About fifteen minutes into the workout, the rug of consciousness was pulled from underneath me, and I dropped to the ground. Upon arrival at the hospital, the last thing I remember was seeing my fiancé enter my room. Then it was "lights out" for the next month. This was the exact moment the trajectory of my life again changed forever, and that feared curse reared its ugly head once again.

I had suffered a ruptured brain aneurysm and was within hours of dying. The next day I had an eight-hour surgery to clamp the aneurysm. My family was told it would be six months to a year to rehabilitate physically, but I accomplished it in two months. Embracing the experience of physical therapy, I enjoyed being challenged. The culture of that therapy room was one of encouragement, support, and celebration of achievements. But once that supportive community of PT ended, I felt truly alone, the same way I had after Carl's death.

I was rehabilitated physically, but what about mentally? I could not go back to work or drive, so I was at home by myself with my mind trying to grasp and understand what the h*ll just happened over the past three months. I was beginning to seek my own answers, trying to figure out why this happened to me. My life has just been turned upside down *again*.

Hey! I just got *engaged*. What about 2021 being my year? WTF?!

The downward mental spiral began again. I am ashamed to say that my alcohol intake played a compelling role in my behavior. I thought alcohol was my friend as it helped me forget the series of traumatic and life-altering events I had been cursed with. Why did God choose to leave me on this earth, only to be knocked down again and again? Was I a horrible person in a past life? Sure, I made bad decisions in this life that God would not approve, and I own up to those, but couldn't He just have sent me straight to hell when I died?

I began to think maybe I should die and just put a stop to being God's punching bag for the rest of my life. There really was no need for me to get married and have my husband become witness to my curse. I knew that was the chickensh*t way out, but I could not find any other way.

I soon developed terrible panic attacks that freaked out my loved ones. These attacks captured my mind and would not let go. They would possess me, and I begged my fiancé to help me kill myself. I wanted him to put me out of my misery so he would not have to observe my dramatic mental episodes. At that point, I started to think I needed professional help.

But I needed that humiliating "drop to my knees" event to convince me to get my sh*t together and take the actions needed to end this curse. To become the strong woman who could pull herself out from under a divine curse, I realized I needed to stop acting like the victim of my circumstances and become the woman God needed me to be. I felt shame, guilt, and embarrassment because of my psychotic behavior that night in Chicago. My behavior was fueled by alcohol, and my fiancé felt helpless, anxiously hoping we would not get kicked out of that hotel.

I honestly still do not understand what triggered my irrational behavior. My mindset clearly needed to shift considerably and quickly. So, through therapy and taking stock of what really matters in life, I decided that optimism and concentrating on helping others would be my way to heal. I made a pact with myself to post an inspiring and motivating message on my Facebook timeline every day for a month. It would not consume much of my time, and maybe I could spread a little positivity.

I received so many positive reactions telling me, "Oh Kelly, I needed to see this today." It sparked something in me to inspire others, in addition to helping myself. That commitment, in turn, empowered me to investigate becoming a life coach. I am proud to say that I am now a certified life coach and for the rest of my life I will have the tools to deal with challenges that will certainly still be coming to me.

Now I know that I am not cursed. Now I have a resilience and inner strength that give me the confidence to embrace this next chapter in my life. I overcame what I thought would be impossible: I did the inner work to get out of the curse mindset. Now I help empower women to tap into their inner strength on their own hero's journey of life.

Kelly Godar is a certified health and life coach, and a certified Clarity Catalyst trainer. The Clarity Catalyst program was developed from a business creativity course for a master's degree at Stanford University. It uses mindfulness and emotional intelligence tools and techniques and is touted as one of the most transformational courses ever to be taught at Stanford. Kelly is happily married and resides in St. Louis, Missouri. She spent twenty-five years successfully managing her father's small family business, learning it from the ground up. As the founder of Empowerment Coaching 4U, LLC, she helps women cultivate their resilience and embark on a journey of self-discovery and empowerment. Her clients achieve their goals and live a more balanced and fulfilling life.

Pam Kueker

Grief Bakes a Cake

Life can be so cruel. One minute everything is just fine, and then fate decides to put your world through a tailspin. Suddenly you find yourself in this terrible storm, tossing you in every direction, leaving you battered, bruised, and broken. You have to decide what to do afterward: Are you going to let life continue to toss you around, or are you going to swim out of the storm?

The day my world fell apart started as a normal day. My kids went to school and my husband and I both went to work. Every day on my way to work I talked to my mom, my confidante. On this day, however, I had things on my mind and needed to focus on my work day, so I cut my morning conversation with her short. That decision remains my biggest regret in life.

That afternoon, I got the call from my daughter that my mom, who *always* picked the kids up from school, was not there. She was *never* late. I was certain this meant something was wrong with her. After making a ton of calls and sending texts to her with no response, I knew I had to leave work and go find her, despite the hour-long drive back home.

That hour was the longest of my life, as my panic led me to visualize every possibility. By the time I arrived at her home, the reality of the situation was setting in. My husband had seen on social media that an accident was reported on the route she drove every day to pick up the kids. I just *knew* that was her, so I started praying, begging God to keep her safe and protect her. I reached out to a friend who helped me figure out what was happening, and she was there with me when the coroner arrived to deliver the news to my dad and me.

Mom was hit head-on by a teenage driver who crossed the yellow line. Mom died instantly. The only other information he could share at that time was that she did not suffer.

I never imagined how the moment of losing my mom would feel. I certainly never imagined it would be this early in our lives, or feel like I, myself, was dying. I was devastated. A vice in my chest squeezed my heart and lungs. Then a dagger ripped them out of my body. Remaining standing took every ounce of my strength. I remember looking at my dad and he was just frozen, like a film on pause.

And then my mind exploded with thoughts. *I can't live this life without her. How will I know the right thing for my kids without her wise advice? I can't keep working so far from home … Who will pick up the kids from school?*

I started calling to inform family members. I thought I couldn't be any more devastated, but now I had to tell others that she was gone.

Mom was not just my hero; she was everyone's hero. The matriarch of the family, she kept us all together, sometimes at a cost—her own anxiety. Without any conscious awareness, I started filling those shoes. I knew someone had to take care of Dad, so I ensured all the funeral arrangements went smoothly and that everyone was where they needed to be. I planned for Dad to be looked after throughout the funeral.

No one told me how incapacitated I'd be for days after the funeral: depressed, exhausted. I wanted nothing more than for the phone to ring and to hear Mom's voice. I wanted to disappear from the world. Honestly,

Pam Kueker | Grief Bakes a Cake

I wanted to stop existing. I knew that putting the pieces of my life back together would take some time, but I had no idea where to start.

My mom was "my person"—that one person I could tell anything to and she would listen, support, and not judge. I knew that to survive, finding a new "person" was a must. So I searched for a therapist well versed in grief and loss and was blessed to find an amazing one. Not only did she understand the pain of my grief but she knew exactly how to let me feel all the emotions of grief. She sat with me in my darkest days. She helped me process my pain and understand it as appropriate.

God had set me up to be surrounded by people who truly cared as I felt the darkest pain in my life. Frankly, I didn't always appreciate that support, simply because these caring people were not Mom, and her support was what I needed most.

Even with all this support, I spent a lot of time feeling lost and empty inside. Music was usually my solace, but losing Mom took away my love of music. I didn't want to celebrate Christmas that year—it just wasn't Christmas without her. I tried to keep going to church, but somehow it didn't feel the same. I literally didn't step foot in my church for several months. I just wasn't motivated. I didn't understand why God would take her away from me at a time in my life when I needed her the most. Why would He do that to me? What had I done to deserve this?

I was angry, it's true; but I didn't know who I was angry at. I couldn't be mad at the other driver—she was so young and had to live the rest of her life knowing she took a life. A part of me was mad at myself that I cut that last phone call short out of my own selfishness. Why did I not put her first at that moment? I talked to my therapist about feeling abandoned, but even that was hard to explain because I didn't think Mom would ever abandon me and my kids. And I could never believe that God would abandon me. Or did He?

After about a year of deep, dark grief and depression, God proved He had not. He brought me an angel. A woman at my church who was a member of the choir reached out and invited me to join the choir. She knew I enjoyed music (or at least that I used to), and I had known her my whole life. I accepted the invitation, but it took a few months for me to finally show up—and ironically it was at Lent, a season of repentance.

One day I was speaking to a neighbor of my dad's. She had just lost a pregnancy and was also grieving. I thought I could sit with her the way my friends and therapist sat with me, but this act became my Aha! moment. Her husband is a preacher, and she was so at peace knowing that God had not forsaken her. And then I realized I *was* angry at God. The feeling of abandonment was that I felt abandoned by God.

I finally admitted this insight to my therapist, and saying it aloud gave me the opportunity to start a journey back to God—and to my love of music. That Lenten season was the most profoundly healing experience of my life. I spent those forty days praying and asking God for peace and forgiveness. I spent much time with the choir ladies, listening to their faith stories and excitement for singing praise to God. I discovered God sent those ladies to my life; they were *all* my angels on Earth. They brought me back to Him.

From that point forward, and every day since, I have focused my life on faith in God. This refocusing allowed me to start living a better life for my family and to find a new source for my energy and passion. I had to rely on God to show me this energy and passion. And that is how I found the courage to reclaim that "one thing" that helped me feel peace: baking. Mom loved baking, and many of the memories of my childhood that I share with my kids now include baking with her.

So now, baking gives me peace. When I bake something, I feel Mom's presence in my life, and this peaceful activity has become my new energy and passion.

I will never know why I lost my mom when and how I did. At this point, I don't want to know. I still miss her with every breath I take. But instead of letting my grief sink me, I chose to swim through it and find a new version of myself. The most important lesson learned is that it is OK to be sad, and when the time is right, it is also OK to find joy amidst your darkness.

That joy kept my life-light shining, and that is definitely what my loved ones want. I am certain Mom would also not want me to be full of darkness. She would want me to live my light as a celebration of all the love and wisdom she gave me during her short time as my mom. That certainty is the magic ingredient in the cake grief baked with my life.

Pam Kueker spent fifteen years as a social worker whose mission was to assist children and families in living their best lives. That mission was interrupted by tragedy when her mother was killed in a car accident, and she left her career behind to focus on her family. Being fully present for them allowed Pam the time to embark on a journey to heal her grief. This difficult journey also led her to follow her heart, creating peace and joy in a way that her mother taught her. To honor her mom's memory, Pam opened a cottage baking business, PJ's Custom Cake Creations, where she bakes for others with pure love, just as her mother taught her.

Jenn Cobbel

Bottom of the Barrel

Military deployments carry challenges not seen by people with no affiliation to the military. One significant impact is that the spouse becomes a single parent—not by choice or through abandonment, but by duty to our country.

When Dave and I married in December of 1999, he was already in the Navy, and I was the boot camp girlfriend. We had already experienced a long-distance relationship, but I was about to learn that deployments add other layers of difficulty to the distance.

After the wedding, we had two weeks before Dave headed to a base in Japan that would be our first duty station, and from there leave on a three-month deployment. While Dave was deployed, I lived with my parents and packed all our belongings to prepare for the very long boat ride to Japan. I thought, *If this is what deployment is like … I got this!* But I was twenty-two and had no clue.

A few days after Dave returned to Japan from that deployment, over the ocean I moved, with my one-way ticket to the rest of my life. I was excited to see Dave, ready to really start our married life. But that young girl had no idea what was coming next.

I arrived at Narita International Airport, where Dave met me. We shared the same excitement: after ninety plus days of being apart, we were finally together. I think everyone in the airport knew we were newlyweds.

Once back in the house Dave had found for us, we settled in, and then ... his question surprised me. "You remember how to get to base and the little grocery store down the street?" Wait, what? He was leaving already? He'd just gotten home after three months!

For the next year, Dave was home for two days and gone for four weeks. Home for three days and gone for two weeks. Home for a day and gone for a month. This cycle went on for what seemed forever. Meanwhile, I was at our house in Japan and alone.

At first that alone time was kind of cool. I put away everything from my suitcases, organized the house, and slept a lot. Then the loneliness set in. I was in a foreign county by myself, with no phone, no TV, no friends, and no family. The one person I knew best and loved most was not there with me. I cried a lot.

Loneliness is difficult for everyone, and especially for someone like me who is an extremely social person, a social butterfly. From living a life filled with friends and family always around, I now knew not a soul, and not a soul knew me.

After the first couple of deployments, one of the other wives came over to the house and invited me to her house for dinner. I didn't know her at all, only that her husband was in the same band with Dave. With hesitation, I went for dinner.

That one dinner ended my loneliness. My hostess had also invited some of the other wives from the same band. All of them had kids, and they could see how lonely I was. These experienced Navy wives quickly took me under their wings, showed me around the area where we lived, and introduced me to making my way on my own, and that helped make my loneliness less lonely.

That one dinner not only changed my lonely life at that station, but it also changed how I looked at the world and other people. They showed me that even though we are alone, we don't have to be. Friends turn into family.

We all started getting orders to new duty stations. Houses packed up, suitcases made ready, and then came the last hand wave. With the first of many farewells, I learned that in military families there are never any "goodbyes," only "see you later." You never realize how much a friendship means to you until you have to say "See you later" without any certainty that you will.

Our friends' kids grew up, and Dave and I had Bailey. She was born in Japan, in the middle of a typhoon, while Dave was gone on deployment. My two favorite friends were there with me. One of them should have been home with her family cleaning their house because they were leaving Japan the next day. Yet there she was with me, in the hospital, holding my hand and coaching me through labor while I was on the phone with Dave.

Navy families move every two to five years. A couple of moves later, we are in Port Hueneme, California, and Dave has changed his job in the Navy. Now he is a Seabee, and they are deployed to not so fun places, like Iraq and Afghanistan, aka *the sandy pit*. And Seabee deployments are long—seven to ten months long—with added prep time and off-base field exercises beforehand.

You would think that after a few moves and the way the ladies in Japan brought me in under their wing that this new life would be a walk in the park. This perspective is common among non-military folks—that although you move all the time, you know someone everywhere you go. It is not true, really, until you have been with the military for twenty years or more.

Dave, Bailey, and I had been in California for only three months before his next deployment with the Seabees. Then Bailey and I were alone, without Papa Dave for eight months. Now, if you are thinking "She has done this before" or "This shouldn't be hard for her anymore," you are wrong. By then, I had become that single parent who is both mom and dad, dog walker, poop picker-upper, cook, cleaner, and the general manager who keeps the cars maintained, pays the bills, helps with homework, keeps myself put together, and is a rock for Bailey. All of this was exhausting. I needed *my* rock to lean on, *my* shoulder to cry on. My rock was halfway around the world making our country a safe place for everyone who lives here.

The first two to three weeks of every deployment were the same. I slept on the couch because I couldn't sleep alone in our bed. I cried a lot when Bailey was at kindergarten. No laundry washed, dishes piling up in the kitchen, the house wasn't cleaned. I couldn't go to the grocery store, so we survived on what was in the house.

I called this early-weeks condition the deployment funk. But let's be real here: that was total depression.

After those two or three weeks of just nothing, there would be a day when I'd wake up and say to myself, *Enough is enough; find the routine.*

The first routine was small, maybe showering and starting some laundry. That's it. That's all my body and mind would let me do. As the next few weeks went on, more and more activities found their way back into my day. The one that always took the longest was sleeping in our bed. About four months into these deployments, I would finally find comfort sleeping in our bed because I knew we were halfway to Dave being home with us again. By this halfway mark, I was beginning to get out of the funk and get into the groove of life again.

The groove of life. That sounds so easy. The struggle with depression is real, no matter what form it comes in. Doing little things can either be what pushes me forward or sends me three steps back. I tried doing those little things that would push me forward, that would give me that momentum to keep going. It didn't always work but often helped.

From my community of support, I learned four significant lessons. First, there really is no "goodbye," only "see you later." Secondly, your "family" doesn't have to be blood relatives. Third, yes, there are lows, like the *extreme* bottom below the false bottom of the barrel. Finally, I learned that when I find my routine, resilience comes with it. That strength might be slow to rise and seem too small to matter, but it does get me there. I'm proud to say I have been surprised by the power I have found in myself along the way.

Jenn Cobbel is a speaker on women's leadership and empowerment who lives in Glen Carbon, Illinois, with her husband, Dave, retired from the United States Navy after twenty-three years as a Chief Equipment Operator. They have two beautiful daughters and two fur babies.

Jenn graduated from Southern Illinois University at Edwardsville with a Bachelor of Science in Music Performance. She has performed with St. Louis Youth Symphony, St. Louis Symphony, Tokyo Symphony, Waukegan Symphony, and Chicago Philharmonic, and taught students on bassoon, flute, and piano.

After significant volunteer positions as Navy Ombudsman and working as a museum gift shop manager, Jenn is now Director of Operations with Advisors at Northwestern Mutual. She volunteers with her neighborhood homeowner's association and the parent-teacher organization at her daughters' school. Jenn is also active in Edwardsville Rotary, Ladies Auxiliary at the American Legion in Glen Carbon, Women Empowering Woman of Edwardsville, and Little Black Book of Southern Illinois–Madison County.

Katie Gearin

No Longer Silent: The Journey to Finding My Voice

The month was February, and the day was dark and gloomy. *Typical*, I thought, as rain poured down and cracks of thunder ricocheted throughout the small, cramped hallway of the old college building. The setting was like something out of Poe, and I felt about as unsettled as the narrator in *The Fall of the House of Usher* as I braved the way toward the door to my classroom.

This type of discomfort may be expected in a university student, but it certainly sets a bad example when it lives in the professor. My reason for the dramatic feeling of impending doom was that this was what felt like a fatal day: my mentor would be observing my teaching.

The moment of truth finally arrived after that hour and fifteen minutes ended, and my mentor sat down with me to discuss my performance. My fear had not prepared me for the shock of her actual words. She said I was a *natural* with a poised, self-assured, and easygoing manner that she seldom saw in young teachers. She added how it was shocking that this was only my first semester teaching.

Poised, self-assured, and easygoing? Years before, I would not have envisioned those characteristics as mine. In fact, I never would have guessed I'd willingly enter a profession that required public speaking.

As a teenager, nothing terrified me more than speaking in public. Like many young women, I had crippling self-esteem issues that left me feeling inadequate and inferior. My low self-esteem led me down dark paths of depression, body dysmorphia, and disordered eating patterns. However, the worst repercussion was the feeling of a complete lack of direction in life. Where does one plan to go when they think they are nothing? How does one plan for their future when they are so displeased and distrustful with their present self? The journey to finding my voice and purpose has been a surprising one full of several twists and turns, complete with an unanticipated cast of players who took my hand and helped me navigate my uncertainties.

The deadly poison that kills self-esteem and fuels anxiety is worrying about what other people think of you. This toxin is something I have struggled with for as long as I can remember. It can be easy to say you don't care what others think, but it is much harder to rewire your brain to accomplish this task. Something that deeply bothered me while I was in high school was the social stigma surrounding my homeschooling. Whenever I revealed to people that I was homeschooled, there was always a look of surprise/disgust followed by possibly well-meaning—but nevertheless insulting—comments.

I collected these comments like some people collect Pokémon. Here are some that hurt deeply then but now appear funny: *Do you have any friends besides your family? Will you ever go to a real school? How will you prepare for college? Does your mom automatically give you straight As?* When I was fifteen, my stern and judgmental pediatrician bluntly remarked, *Do you actually do any work?*

Most of these comments had one theme in common: they all assumed something about my intelligence. It did not seem to matter that my curriculum was from an accredited school in Virginia and that licensed teachers graded all my work. What mattered was I was not living out the "normal" high school experience, which indicated that my academic successes would never be significant.

Instead of challenging people's ignorant assumptions about my intelligence, I internalized them. Growing up I always thought that I was not pretty or skinny enough. Now I could also add not being *smart* enough to my list of insecurities.

Since I believed I wasn't smart, I lacked all ambition. The sole career I could settle on was cosmetology, but I didn't choose this career for the correct reasons. While I loved doing my own hair and makeup, the main attraction was not needing a college degree. Considering that I thought I was not smart enough to attend college, this seemed like the safest option.

My parents were more enthusiastic when looking at my future and recommended that I go to the nearby community college. While I was incredibly doubtful, I didn't want to disappoint them. At the time, starting college felt like a death sentence. Today I recognize that saying yes to college was the beginning of the journey to finding my voice.

But it didn't immediately start out wonderful. For the first semester of college, I stopped menstruating. When the doctors finally stopped challenging my testimony that I wasn't pregnant, they concluded that it was extreme stress. And stressed out I most assuredly was. For years I had listened to people question my intelligence and worth. Despite the stress and constant fear that everyone would see how worthless I was, a strange thing happened.

I spoke up in my classes. In my English 101 class, I felt uncomfortably sympathetic when my teacher asked a question and silence descended upon the classroom. To help her, I spoke up and expressed my opinions about the reading. The best part was that no one ever laughed, and my teacher was always grateful for my participation and leadership. My involvement in that English class soon spread to other classes.

In my American History class, I vividly remember the day when each student had to bring their research paper rough drafts to the teacher's desk for review. I can still feel the nervous tension as we stood by the desk in a row. Controlling my muscles created an excruciating tension, as I ensured that my classmates could not see my legs or hands shaking. At my turn to present my paper to the teacher, I held my breath. Then I felt absolute astonishment when she loudly proclaimed that it was wonderful and exactly what she wanted for the essay.

As I walked back to my little table, with all my classmates' eyes on me in pure wonderment, I felt like Miss America. This was my first research paper in college, and I had been dreading it. As I was writing, I was sure that every word was wrong. Receiving positive feedback and recognition on that small assignment was one of the major turning points in my life.

The feedback on that research paper made me realize that I was good at something. This startling fact indicated that I needn't settle for a no-college career. With my newfound confidence, I sought out more writing-intensive classes. My enthusiasm did not go unnoticed; teachers were wonderful in their encouragement and nudged me toward declaring a major in English. By the time I graduated with my associate's degree, I had a new goal. Perhaps it was the first real goal in my life: to pursue a career in English.

That decision culminated in earning a master's degree. While in higher education, I held jobs as a writing tutor, a graduate instructor, and a research assistant. I discovered my love for tutoring and teaching because of the satisfaction of helping anxious students. When I compliment a student who clearly hasn't received validation before and remark that they have a knack for writing, my heart swells with joy at their ecstatic expression.

My experiences helping students contribute to my satisfaction in a job that does not pay well and affords little societal respect. I feel privileged to be a part of someone's journey to finding their voice, and I do all I can to encourage them. In doing so, I not only help them but also heal that little girl in me who felt she was not good enough.

Obviously, I did not make it to cosmetology school, although I still spend a ridiculous amount of time on my hair and makeup. Instead, a myriad of professions as an English professor, writing tutor, and freelance editor have filled my life. A few months after I graduated with my master's degree, I returned to my old community college, this time as a member of the faculty. As I walk the halls of the place where I was once a student, I sometimes get emotional. When I pass my old English teachers in the hallway, my heart accelerates, and I pass by quickly with a shy smile on my face. I imagine this as the reaction I would feel seeing a celebrity. I look forward to the day when I have the courage to go up to my former teachers and talk with them about how much they changed my life.

In reflecting on my journey, I'm reminded of a quote by Madeleine Albright in an interview from what was then *The Huffington Post*. Thinking over her career, she remarked, "It took me quite a long time to develop a voice, and now that I have it, I'm not going to be silent."[1] While it took me "only" ten years to find my voice, that certainly seemed like "quite a long time." Like Albright, I am also determined not to remain silent anymore and, in the words of another feminist icon, Ruth Bader Ginsberg, to say what I'm feeling even if "my voice is shaking."[2]

And shake it sometimes still does. The journey to finding my voice may be over, but the journey to feel comfortable using it continues. I still occasionally feel nervous when sitting in a work meeting. Questions such as *What if what I contribute is stupid?* still pervade my mind and hinder my speech. While my insecurities are certainly not gone for good, what is different is the way I respond to them. I do not succumb to the anxiety and let it paralyze me. Instead of dwelling on negative emotions, thus allowing them to hold me back, I use them as fuel to propel me forward.

I strive to be like literary heroine Elizabeth Bennet and let my courage arise with every attempt to intimidate me.[3] Now, I am building a network of people who will have my back, support me, and lead me in the right direction. I also remind myself daily that nobody is perfect and that my occasional feelings of inadequacy are temporary. I will not always feel strong and may occasionally sink back down to the low depths of self-esteem, but I no longer remain there.

Now, I have the tools to rise and come back more powerful than ever before … and so do you. History shows us the challenges women face when seeking confidence and success in the world. However, history is also full of reminders that women are tough, resilient, and ready to rise to the challenge.

Endnotes
1 Marianne Schnall, "Madeleine Albright: An Exclusive Interview." *The Huffington Post,* June 15, 2010. https://www.huffpost.com/entry/madeleine-albright-an-exc_b_604418
2 Shari Graydon, "Four Lessons from the Life and Advocacy of Ruth Bader Ginsberg." *Informed Opinions.* https://informedopinions.org/four-lessons-from-the-life-and-advocacy-of-ruth-bader-ginsburg/
3 Austen, Jane. *Pride and Prejudice.* Sterling Publishing Co., Inc., 2012.

Katie Gearin | No Longer Silent: The Journey to Finding My Voice

Katie Gearin is a writing tutor and adjunct English professor at St. Charles Community College, as well as a freelance editor who frequently collaborates with Davis Creative Publishing Partners. A native of St. Charles, Missouri, she holds an associate's degree in Arts and Sciences from St. Charles Community College, a bachelor's in English from Maryville University, and a master's in English from St. Louis University. In her free time, Katie likes to spend time with her two dogs, Daisy and Belle, read (especially literature from the nineteenth century), watch classic movies, and talk to anyone who will listen about anything related to Broadway.

Dr. Jennifer Capler

Reflections

A spritz of my perfume tickled my nose and caught my attention. My reflection in the bathroom mirror revealed a sly smirk and the start of definition lines on the cheeks.

When was the last time I put on perfume?

When was the last time I saw definition in my cheeks?

When was the last time I truly felt amazing about myself?

In life, people are presented with many obstacles that are opportunities for change. We can become stronger, or we can self-destruct. What happens when one obstacle creates both? When my world imploded, it launched a long journey of reflection and change. Grief will do that to a person.

As I write, more than two and a half years have passed since my husband Carl died unexpectedly from a brain aneurysm. June 11, 2021, created a permanent scar on my heart. It also spurred me to reflect upon who I was, what I wanted, and where I wanted my life to go. It has been one h*ll of a journey. And now our youngest child is graduating high school. For the first time in twenty-seven years, I will be responsible for only me.

My husband was a pillar of support for me. When he died, I felt broken and lost. My anchor was gone, leaving me to drift in a turbulent ocean of chaos. Before he died, Carl provided significant support for my achievements: Doctor of Management in Organizational Leadership, a published researcher and author, and a business owner.

Carl was a part of me, and I was a part of Carl. Together, we were one. And then suddenly, half of me was gone.

That's the thing about an amazing relationship. Two live as one. From hard times, we came out stronger, together. He wasn't always the best father, but he was an amazing husband. Carl was working toward sharing with our adult children how his past affected his behavior as a dad. Because he never got the chance, I honored his intention to share, opening a new perspective for our children about how much their father worked on being a better person.

After Carl's death, I spent months in an absolute haze of conversations I barely remember. I was conscious, but it was my subconscious mind that kept me functioning, zombie-like. I knew I had bills to pay and a teenager to care for, and I did the bare minimum to function before curling back into myself, hiding from my new reality.

As I neared the end of the grief haze, I fell into partying and drinking. I went on a cruise to the Southern Caribbean, creating new friendships and experiencing a brief, steamy relationship. Seeking to numb myself from the pain, sorrow, anger, and shock of loss, I was forced to confront my feelings while suffering hangovers.

And I hid from the world. When I had to interact with people, I put on a fragile mask and pretended I was OK. People came and went, with only a few sticking around for the long haul. I was intentionally keeping people at arm's length, building a barrier between myself and a much-needed support network.

All of 2022 and the first half of 2023, I paid bills, performed work, and did whatever needed to be done. I existed, while holding on to my fragile mask. And life continued: I was appointed a position with my local government and asked to join a band. I did it all half-heartedly, still broken.

I started writing a memoir about life after Carl's death but put it off because I didn't know how it ended. How could I write about relief beyond pain when I was still deep in grief?

By the last half of 2023, life was also physically painful. My back hurt all the time, restricting movement. I suffered heat exhaustion, so summer's heat prevented healthy walks. I was packing on weight, eating more as an attempt to numb my crummy feelings, while still hiding from the world. Clinging to the idea that I was moving forward in my new normal, I couldn't see I was falling into a pit of pain and despair.

Mid-November 2023 delivered the mega slap upside the head that spurred change and action: Type 2 diabetes and insanely horrid cholesterol levels.

Embarrassed and ashamed by the depth of the pit I had dug myself into, I only told my children and my mother. Now I knew I wasn't just lying to everyone else about being fine; I was lying to myself. Still deeply grieving for Carl, I offered a good performance for spectators and for the woman staring back at me in the mirror. But I was falling apart under the façade.

Just after Thanksgiving 2023, I made the conscious and subconscious decision to do and be better. It was time to choose to not just live, but to thrive. It was time to decide what kind of future I wanted.

My conscious decision to take control of my health was coordinated with my doctor. The first step was a medication to help my scary cholesterol levels, which were far more concerning than my barely registering on the diabetes scale. The second step was to limit my intake of refined sugars and simple carbs and to begin tracking my blood sugar levels.

My doctor advised seeing a physical therapist and starting a workout routine to help with my lower back pain. It was slow going and painful at first, but I started with two to three days per week of cardio or muscle toning. Within two months, I started looking forward to working out and my back was feeling better. I saw the numbers on my scale drop morning after morning. The mirror showed my body slimming. My clothes became more comfortable to wear.

For the first time in my entire life, I enjoyed the euphoric feeling of finishing a sweat-inducing workout. My conscious and subconscious were in alignment to improve my health and my life. I shifted my business to focus on my writing, building a desired future. I once believed those who'd predicted failure as I followed my dreams and what I wanted … until now. Now, I am the only person who will decide what my dreams are and how I achieve them.

And now, a simple gift of perfume from my oldest child stopped me in my tracks. As I gazed upon my reflection, I pondered: When was the last time I truly felt sexy in my own skin? When have I felt worthy of creating the life I wanted? Of creating a future for myself?

Can I honestly say that I am fully healed from Carl's death? Yes and no. Grief is a fickle beast that each person learns to tame on their own terms and in their own time. The tides of grief continue like ocean waves upon a shore, but the surf is far gentler now.

Today, the smell of perfume on my skin triggers an avalanche of feeling I am good enough, I am sexy, and I can (and *will*) be what I want to be. While grieving and pretending I was better than I really was, I had still set a path for my future. I am a writer. I am a singer in a band. I am the City Clerk. I am a board member. I am a business owner. And I lowered my bad cholesterol (LDL) from 168 points to 72 points in only a couple of months while also decreasing my A1c by 0.1.

These days, I add perfume and earrings regardless of what I'm wearing. I work out at least five days per week: muscle definition, toning, or aerobics. I eat far more fruits and vegetables than ever before. And I feel good as I gaze at my reflection.

Now, it's a daily practice to go to the mirror and look myself in the eyes. I tell myself that I *am* a bad*ss sexy b*tch. I am a writer. I am an author. I am a singer. I am everything I want to be, and more. And I look d*mn good doing it!

Dr. Jennifer Capler | Reflections

Dr. Jennifer Capler is the Word Slinger and owner of The DM Woman, LLC, a singer in Mark & The Angry Heart, a board member, an elected official, and a veteran of the US Navy. She loves working with words, whether it's grant writing, content writing, book writing, or editing and proofreading. She is a published researcher and author, with her first memoir, *Transformation through Life, Love, and Death: A Widow's Journey To and Through Grief*, releasing in the second half of 2024. A woman always on the go, she enjoys strolling through nature, paranormal investigations, travel, and getting in her workouts. When she's not on the go, Jennifer can be found leisurely sipping her coffee, reading a steamy novel, or binging her latest movie fixation. Jennifer has entered the stage of life where she is discovering the joy of living life for herself and doing whatever she so chooses.

Heather Calvin

I Am Not a Piece of Sh*t

A childhood filled with abuse, negativity, and financial hardship left me with low self-esteem and a belief that I would never achieve financial freedom or success. So when a financial adviser told me and my husband, "You are on track to retire at your goal age of fifty-five," my jaw dropped to the floor.

I was speechless, in disbelief, and could not stop myself from nervous laughter. We were forty-nine and fifty years old, both from humble beginnings, and twenty-three years before this moment we had been in financial ruins. We had lost our house and started over, from scratch, with two kids and a dog. If at any point in my life prior to that moment you had asked if I would be able to retire that young, I would have laughed and exclaimed, "I wish!"

You see, my childhood was riddled with negativity at home, at school, and everywhere else I went—neighbors, church. To sum it up, abuse was the norm in my world: verbal, emotional, physical, and sexual. "You don't know anything, you are not good enough, you won't ever amount to anything, you are a piece of sh*t …" The words changed but gave that same message every day.

And I believed I was a piece of sh*t. I was never smart enough, never good enough, and according to "him" I was never going to be. Messages of poverty were mixed with the abuse; my family was lower middle class at best. The phrases "we don't have a pot to piss in or a hand to hold it in" and "robbing Peter to pay Paul" were frequent in our household. We went to the free clinic for our medical needs and often visited the food pantry for our meals. Any financial prosperity visible from the outside was a mirage, as we kids benefited from church scholarships for most everything. Clothing came from church family hand-me-downs. Food baskets delivered by the church fed our family home for the holidays. At school I was bullied and beaten up daily, for, you see, I was small, short, and skinny.

To say I had no self-esteem and that my self-talk was negative was an understatement! I had many failed relationships as a teenager and young adult, which only added insult to injury. I missed sixty-four days of my senior year of high school because I had no idea who I was, who I wanted to be, and absolutely no idea what I wanted to do with my life. All I had ever known was survival mode, which does not empower the mental capacity to dream about what you want in life.

Somehow, I did graduate high school on time, and even went on to college. But I dropped out after two months, and then one month later, at the age of nineteen, I got pregnant and had a baby. The first moment I saw her face, I knew I had to do something to overcome my circumstances.

The trauma from abuse, the lack of self-esteem, the negative self-talk, the thoughts that I would never have financial freedom or security … From that moment on, I had to push all that down and focus on the care of this precious child. I had to raise her up and provide her with the best life I could.

I was scared and ashamed that I needed to sign up for aid at the state office; however, it was a necessary step in my journey. I accepted WIC, food stamps, financial aid, testing and grants for college, as well as health insurance. Leveraging these services empowered me to get on my feet and provide for my child. I enrolled at Missouri College and started classes to become a Medical Computer Secretary.

Raising a baby as a full-time student and working to pay all the bills meant I was also full-time exhausted and occasionally hopeless. I was tired, but I had to keep going. Then, in the middle of my eighteen-month school program, I received a diagnosis of precancerous cells on my cervix and had to undergo an extremely scary and painful loop electrosurgical excision procedure. One of the school's requirements was that I could not miss class, so I had to push through. I graduated with academic honors, a huge accomplishment after all my Cs and Ds in high school.

All through this overwhelmingly busy, frightening passage of my life, my attitude of perseverance served me well. Regardless of what new challenge life threw into my path, I simply took a deep breath and forged ahead. My baby relied on me for everything, and her future was my motivation to go on when going on seemed impossible. I embraced the point of view that I could not allow myself to fail.

At twenty, I met the love of my life; we were married after sixteen months and had a son three years later. We both worked but could not afford child care, so we worked opposite shifts, and each parented the kids while the other worked. This schedule was challenging and exhausting. We were both working overtime to bring in enough income for all our expenses and still missing that mark each month. And it was not like we were living an extravagant lifestyle. We lived in a mobile home, drove used cars, owned cheap or secondhand furniture. Making barely over minimum wage, we had made bad decisions to borrow money through high-interest personal loans. We had bill collectors relentlessly calling and banging on the front door wanting their money. We had nothing to give them.

Distraught and feeling like a failure, I thought, "he" *was* right. I did not know anything, I was not good enough, I had not amounted to anything, I was a piece of sh*t.

It's interesting how all that past trauma and negativity rearing its ugly head when I was at my lowest moments in life helped me rationalize the negative self-talk. I did not have the time or luxury, though, to entertain that line of thinking for long. We had to figure out a way to survive.

After we lost our house, we moved from Missouri to Illinois, from the mobile home we had been buying to an empty mobile home that was already paid for. We did what we could to make this new start work for us. We determined we would not ever again end up in financial ruin. We started spending cash only, no credit cards, no loans. We contributed to our two 401(k)s and lived modestly. To save the expense of child care, I stopped working full time until our kids were in school full days. When our son turned five, I shifted back to full-time employment after those years of watching kids at the house and doing odd jobs around town.

In the corporate workforce, one of my main objectives was to make more money. Always looking for ways to advance my career, my sole purpose of *earning more* drove my ambition. I kept going so we could pay our bills and improve our lives, as well as our children's lives.

Promoted to supervisor at a customer service company, I struggled to develop my direct reports. I often vented to my manager about how my team did not want to learn, grow, develop, or do better. My manager offered suggestions, and I kept replying, "I know; I tried that; it's not me." One day he looked directly at me and said, "I cannot help you." I was confused and blurted, "What?" He yelped, "If you are not willing to hear constructive criticism and act on it, then I cannot help you. If you think you know everything, then I cannot help you."

This wake-up call invited me to open my eyes to some hard realities. Upon reflection, I realized he was right. I was *not* receptive to his constructive criticism and advice. Thinking with an open mind about his advice and putting it into action helped me begin to truly succeed in my role. For example, I learned that leading is about enabling people to do their best work by ensuring they have all the tools and resources they need to succeed. This approach has become a staple in my everyday work both for myself and those I serve.

This new insight from my manager's honesty and my self-reflection was a turning point in my career. Since then, I have been promoted every couple of years, increased my salary and other compensation exponentially, and truly thrived and succeeded. In turn, my career growth contributed to our family's financial freedom. Now I can live my best life, travel extensively both domestic and abroad, and plan for my retirement three years from now, early at the age of fifty-five so that we can enjoy our lives.

So now you know why it was such a shock when our financial adviser confirmed we were on track to retire that early. We had never had a review of our finances prior to that conversation, we did not have a plan, and we did not know what we were doing. How did this happy outcome happen?

I see our ambition, determination, sheer will, and perseverance as the biggest factors; we just kept going, no matter what. And we enabled ourselves through listening and learning, self-reflection, failing, and being accountable for our failures. We disciplined our spending choices, using fact-based decision-making. We put money into our 401(k)s and forgot it; it was not an option to use it before retirement. We stopped taking out loans except for our home and car, purchased everything else with cash, and did not live beyond our means. And because of those choices, we are now living our best lives.

I often look over at my husband and say, "I am so proud of us; look what we did!" I no longer live from that mindset that I am a piece of sh*t destined to live in poverty. I am not a piece of sh*t! And it turns out that "he" was wrong all along.

Heather Calvin | I Am Not a Piece of Sh*t

Heather Calvin is from St. Louis, Missouri, raised her family in Grafton, Illinois, and currently resides in Richmond, Indiana. She has been married to her husband, Eddie, for thirty years. Together they share two children and four grandchildren. She is Director in Provider Strategy and Insights Delivery at United Healthcare, where she has been employed for the last twenty years. When faced with needing to care for her baby and survive financial ruin, she turned to two strategies: 1) financial education and disciplined approaches to spending and saving money; and 2) listening and being coachable at work. Those two major changes helped her overcome the trauma of childhood abuse, negative self-talk, low self-esteem, and financial ruin. Today Heather loves spending time with her family and friends, traveling the United States and abroad, and planning for her retirement in three years.

Jennifer Whitehead

Redefining Success

"I don't know how you do it, Jen."

If I had a dollar for every time I heard that phrase, I'd have raked in a few thousand dollars and could afford my dream car, a new fridge, and one of those vacations every person on Instagram seems to be going on. As a twenty-eight-year-old mom with big dreams, my story was: by day, a super woman; by night, a wife and a mom who was mentally broken, emotionally unstable, hadn't had a haircut in over a year, and should have been in much better shape considering my wardrobe consisted solely of gym clothes. My story wasn't one about success. Not yet.

I had been a typical college graduate who believed stepping into the working world would be easy—that my dream job was just waiting for me. I expected a six-figure salary within two years, marriage, and a mortgage. Reality could not have slapped me harder.

I hated my night-shift jobs that paid hourly with no benefits. I bounced around from position to position, hoping to find that spark of excitement, a meaningful purpose, or even my destiny. Through a staffing agency, I discovered a contract position in my field of study and finally was excited about what I did. I'd always heard that if you kept your head down and worked hard, people would notice. They would see the potential and the value in having you work for their company. So that's what I did.

Meanwhile, my personal life was also looking up. My boyfriend had a fantastic outlook in his career, and he moved up the corporate ladder earning raises and promotions. We got engaged and then married when we were both twenty-five years old. My husband found a new job, and we knew the opportunity could arise for us to relocate. I was still a contract worker who had apparently kept her head down for so long that I was lost in the crowd.

I was ready for change. New beginnings, new dreams.

Just as we were ready to move away, my husband was offered an amazing position that kept us right where we were in our hometown. It seemed time to plant some roots and move out of our apartment. The house hunt began, and we found the perfect starter home. Everything was lining up, except for that dream job of mine. I finally demanded that my agency find me a full-time role, and that's exactly what happened.

I started my new role with a veterinary pharmaceutical company after a few short weeks of a grace period to test my skills. I was instantly in love with the work! I created systems, audited, and trained. I was good at what I did, and I excelled at all of it. This company felt like one I could grow with, helping establish their American market. Had I finally made it? Was this the successful end of my story?

"Tell God your plans and watch Him laugh," the saying goes. Just when these two new jobs and our new home life were falling into routines, we learned we were expecting our first baby. So we built our forever house, made it everything we wanted, and brought our baby boy home in 2017. I counted down every day of my maternity leave as most new mothers do. My biggest internal struggle was knowing I didn't want to go back to work but that I was also not meant to be a stay-at-home mom.

I liked having a purpose at work and going into an office to have human interactions. However, I quickly learned upon my return to work that I was not as "valued" as I had thought. Here I was, again, deciding it was time to look for a new job. This time, I knew my worth.

I landed a good job with a very well-known company that had great benefits and plenty of opportunities for advancement. Our new routines and a new life began. For a couple of years, we were comfortable and saving our money, making sure our son had the life we never did.

My husband and I dreamed of having our own business one day, and having our family be a part of it. However, we could never agree on what exactly our business would be, as we were educated in opposite fields. He was all business, and I was all science; our planning conversations always got pushed to a back burner. We were still only thirty years old and had just found out baby boy number two was on the way. By fall 2020 we were a family of four, and that's when our story radically changed.

The amount of coffee my husband and I drank after having our second child could have been a world record. That little red-headed boy gave us a run for our money. It also gave us a path to business ownership: coffee. It was something we both loved and could agree on, and a product that wasn't going away anytime soon. We did our research and came across a small company unknown to the Midwest. Everything felt right. Before we knew it, our informational meetings turned into a ten-hour road trip to visit headquarters. It was settled; this was what we were going to do. We took a leap of faith, signed our contract, and a month later realized we were expecting baby number three.

The word "crazy" couldn't even begin to touch the journey we were about to embark on—months of meetings and contractors while experiencing pregnancy complications and still working full time. By June of 2022 our baby girl was here, and construction of our shop was in full swing. A couple months later I was trying to juggle being a mom of three with my transition back into the workforce and making sure our shop was still on schedule to open.

It didn't take long before I approached my husband and told him that I didn't feel there was any way I could continue working full time and run a coffee shop on the back end. So we agreed that I would leave and become full-time owner/manager of our new shop. I knew I could do it. I was built for it. I knew it meant excessively long days and working every weekend and holiday. We thought if we could manage all the chaos for a year, we would be in a better position and be able step back and hire a manager to run the day-to-day. And there God was, laughing again.

We opened in December of 2022. Married eight years, with a family that now included a five-year-old, two-year-old, and six-month-old … and we weren't even in our midthirties. But we were doing it. I was doing it. We went through so many obstacles in those first months just learning how a coffee business ran. On the outside, we were successful. We had support and help. On the inside, I was struggling.

I was missing events at the preschool for my eldest, missing big milestones of my middle child, and I had missed two of my youngest's "firsts": seeing Santa and saying her first real word. I saw my kids for a short thirty minutes every night right before I put them to bed. I was never there when they woke up, and they only saw me during the day when they came to the shop.

My mom guilt was *intense*. I was missing more than I had ever imagined. The sacrifices were deep. There were many nights of tears, with my husband encouraging me to keep going. He took on more and more responsibilities, and I couldn't have kept going without him.

It's been over a year since we started our business ownership journey. Is it worth it? To be honest, I don't know. And I think that's OK. There have been many, many lows. We managed to get through challenges I never thought we would survive. We both have missed and sacrificed important moments with our family and jobs.

I think becoming a mom was easier than starting a business. But I love seeing something my husband and I accomplished together at such a young age. I love seeing our community embrace us. I love seeing our children love the shop and be proud to say it belongs to them. Most of all, I love seeing how I have grown.

I have found an inner strength in the working world that I didn't know I possessed. And I have realized I am so much more capable than I ever thought I would be. I don't believe I have yet found that point in my life where I can truly say "I made it." I don't know if this coffee shop is where I will be forever, and I'm OK with that.

My story still isn't about success … at least not success in the career world. Not yet. I've realized that success can be defined in an infinite number of ways as I reflect on the things I do have. My marriage has been going strong for nearly a decade. My children are happy, healthy, and clearly will be making their own mark in this world. I may not have reached the peak of my success, but I am successful.

Jennifer Whitehead | Redefining Success

Jennifer Whitehead is an average woman in her midthirties who is redefining what success means. She's been married to the most patient man in the world for almost ten years, and he's not only her best friend but the only human who knows what she's thinking before she does. Jennifer and John have three kids who never seem to tire, which means their parents are always exhausted. Jennifer believes good moms say bad words, and that weekends are for watching the kids play, drink in hand. Jennifer has adapted to jobs, environments, and lifestyles, and knows more random facts about life than most people. Her little family is her world, and she won't stop trying to achieve more so that they can be proud of who she is.

Aliesha Pollino

Not Stuck, Not Stoppin'!

Standing here typing at my desk, my body feels heavy. There is tightness in my chest. I feel my heart beating in my ears, my fingertips are tingling, and tears are streaming over my quivering lips. The thoughts and emotions of what I have endured on my journey to become this version of myself are dancing through my head. I learned at a young age that each of us only gets one life, and it can be over in the blink of an eye.

So many people allow their pasts to dictate their futures. Past traumas, relationships, failures, or disappointments keep them clinging to the "someday" or "maybe when" narratives. Yet time marches forward, regardless, leaving one with a lifetime of what-if's or regrets. I'm no different. I always knew I wanted to help people, but just four years ago I finally saw the light and awakened to my passion and purpose.

I am a *lighthouse*, a beacon of hope shining bright to guide others out of their darkness. Today I help others heal physically, mentally, emotionally, spiritually, and financially so they can embrace self-love and awaken their ability to dream again. Mind you, I was not always a bold, daring, risk-taker. While I do not wish my past on anyone, I wouldn't change it either. All those experiences shaped me into who I am today.

My life changed forever in April 1999, my freshman year of high school. I was "back home" in Pennsylvania on spring break. My family had relocated to North Carolina almost a year earlier. As a fourteen-year-old girl, it felt an eternity had passed since I saw my family and friends. This was way before cell phones and internet were all the rage. Tons of handwritten letters mailed back and forth with my friends, and now I was finally going to see them. I wanted to see so many people and had only a small window of time.

I was excited to celebrate my fifteenth birthday while I was home as well. My aunt (my mom's sister) who was also my godmother called and stated that she planned a whole day of shopping and a sleepover at her house.

It was early morning when my godmother picked me up, and then we were off to paint the town. We spent a good part of the day car shopping at different dealerships, as she planned to purchase my first car when I turned sixteen. We stopped and had a nice lunch together and caught up on our lives. After lunch we hit the mall. She purchased me a Stetson cowboy hat for my birthday. I was so over the moon about it! Later on, during the drive home, I asked her if she would be mad if I spent time with my friends in the evening instead of spending the night at her house, as we'd previously planned. She smiled and said that was fine. When she pulled into my grandparents' driveway to drop me off, I hopped out of the car, told her I loved her, and said I would see her on Sunday for cake and ice cream.

The next morning, I shot up to a sitting position in my bed as I heard the phone ringing. My whole body could feel that something was wrong. I tried to make sense of what my mom was asking the person on the other end of the phone. Then mom's yelling, crying sobs were bellowing from the kitchen. Something had happened to my godmother, and, honestly, the rest was a blur as we quickly got dressed and went to gather with the rest of our family.

My grandma's house was filled with aunts, uncles, and cousins anxiously pacing for hours as we waited for the police to brief us on the details, but once they did we wished it wasn't true. My godmother had been brutally murdered in her home.

The following weeks were a blur; my fifteen-year-old mind began playing wild stories about the horrific details of her murder. I didn't know how to talk about how I was feeling, and I wasn't the only one who lost someone that day. My entire family was devastated, and no one was coping well. So I kept to myself and continued replaying the stories in my head.

I was *so* mad at God; how could he let something like this happen to such an amazing, caring woman? What if I'd been there as planned? Would I have been able to stop it? Would I have been murdered too? Did they follow us all day? Did they know who I was? Would they come find me someday? Would they have decided not to come to her house if she hadn't been alone? Most of all, though, I wondered, *Why did God spare my life?*

I began having a recurring nightmare that continued for years. Every night the dream started with me against the wall under the narrow counter in her kitchen, watching the struggle with a knife take place in the kitchen. I saw how they forced her up the stairs and into her bedroom. I could never see the two men's faces, but I knew one of them had long hair.

At first I tried to wake up from the nightmare because I didn't want to see what was happening. At one point I began to think that my godmother *wanted* me to see all these details over and over. Like she hoped I would find the missing clue to break the case wide open and bring her killers to justice. I got upset with myself for not being able to have a breakthrough and just see the detail of their faces.

By the age of seventeen, the pain, anger, and fear created a short fuse in me, and I was just mad at the world. I found that instead of trying to talk to someone about my feelings, I began to eat them. Food didn't talk back or ask me to explain all the thoughts and emotions in my head.

I couldn't understand why God had let me live. One day, during one of my many mental chats with my godmother, I felt that she spoke back and emphasized that she didn't want me consumed by my emotions and missing out on life's opportunities. I promised her I would learn to live again. While I didn't have a clue what direction to go, I would start being bold and daring because I only get one life!

The next thirteen years became a whirlwind of risk-taking. I was learning how to do it scared! Failure after failure, I persevered, constantly pushing boundaries and embracing change on my path for self-growth, development, and the desire to make the most of my life. I believe success requires frequent failures. That is how I learn and grow and develop. I only truly fail when I give up.

Despite changing colleges and majors twice, I still graduated with a four-year degree in two and a half years, keeping pace with my peers. I lived in various cities, states, and even ventured overseas. Every time I said, "I'll never do that" or "that will never happen," whatever statement I made using the word *never* inevitably became the next item on my bucket list. While living abroad, I earned my MBA and conquered my fear of sharks, becoming a certified open water diver.

I've been married, divorced, and held various jobs before launching my own business. While building my business, I continued to seek new challenges, from Spartan races to playing women's professional football. Football was an amazing experience, and I would never change the decision to play. In a freak accident, though, I got hurt practicing for a playoff game in June 2016. I knew something was majorly wrong on the inside, although nothing on the outside appeared to be wrong. I fought with the insurance company for more than seventeen months, continuing to push through the pain radiating through my body. I kept telling myself, *Suck it up, buttercup; people are way worse off than you.*

January 2018, at age thirty-three, I hit rock bottom, waking to find I couldn't get out of bed. In that moment my whole life flipped upside down. I felt like I drove my car into a brick wall at one hundred miles per hour. Ultimately, I needed two back surgeries in less than one year and had to learn how to walk again.

I lost my business and had mounds of debt; the bills didn't stop just because I couldn't work. My spirit was broken, and I felt like a complete failure. I felt like a burden to my family and friends who took care of me. The next two years were mostly dark days. I no longer dreamed of a future. Most days my life focused on how to survive the next hour ... or the next ten minutes.

Even after I slammed the door on God when my godmother was murdered, God walked with me, and I was never truly alone. He was always there guiding me and nudging me to change paths, as I took detour after detour. God knew I was strong, determined, hardheaded, and resilient. God put people in my life well before my accident because he knew they would be the connection to the people and things I needed to climb out of the dark pit I would soon be in.

By March of 2020, I was down to my last drop of hope. I had to decide—give up, or fight one more time to learn how to continue making the most of my life despite the cards dealt. I embarked on a health journey in May 2020, and in the beginning I thought it was just another diet. My hope was I would lose some weight and feel better. *Yes,* I lost one hundred and three pounds and ninety-six and a half inches in twelve and a half months. More importantly, I *regained my life.*

I brought my mind on the journey as well and learned how to start healing from everything I used to stuff in a box while saying "I'm fine, everything is fine." I started being intentional with all areas of my life: mindset, habits, how I spend my time, people I spend time with, and how to properly fuel my body. While my body may never heal 100 percent, I am in the best place I have ever been in my whole life—physically, mentally, and emotionally.

Time is now the most valuable thing in my life. The life I yearn for requires that I continue to embrace the obstacles in life despite my fears. In these valleys of challenges and uncertainty, I discover the essence of my true strength, power, and purpose. Every day I wake up with a grateful heart for all the blessings in my life and give thanks that I have another opportunity to boldly pursue my dreams.

Aliesha Pollino, CEO of Pollino Health & Wellness, bestselling author, financial specialist, and public speaker, embodies a unique approach to life. She is a devoted dog mom to Lexie, her spirited Australian shepherd, and takes such pride and joy in her roles as aunt to four nieces and nephews and as godmother to three incredible children. Aliesha is an avid outdoors enthusiast, enjoying activities such as hunting, fishing, and exploring nature, all while nurturing her passion for travel. As a transformational coach, Aliesha has guided thousands of individuals to embark on a journey of mental, physical, emotional, and financial healing, guiding them toward self-love and the rediscovery of their dreams. Aliesha's commitment to self-empowerment, resilience, and personal growth serves as a lighthouse, being a light to inspire others to embark on their journeys so they can learn how to thrive in all areas of their lives too.

Amy Jones

Borderline Angel

"I don't normally do this, but your angel guides insisted." She paused, and I anxiously awaited the message I was about to receive. "You killed yourself in a previous life—actually every life you have had—and you will continue to do so until you learn to let go and move forward." These words, spoken by a psychic medium two years ago, felt like a dagger to my heart.

I've always struggled to find peace from the inner chaos of my own mind. I've had a pattern of engaging in self-sabotaging behaviors. I used drugs to numb my pain, and I would physically harm myself if things became too much for me emotionally. I was also extremely codependent when it came to love and relationships and had very little control over my emotions. They were often brewing underneath the surface, caught between two extremes. I was either sinking into a dark, deep depression, manically exploding, or frozen between these two extremes of my personality. These patterns followed me for years, in every aspect of my life, and I really struggled to find balance.

I was seventeen years old when those strong emotions first became too much for me. I remember it vividly. I was at home, in the middle of writing an English paper on the Palace of Versailles, when I got up and went to the medicine cabinet. I took as many pills as I could find. I sat back down and continued to write my paper before eventually passing out. The next morning, I went to my parents' room and began vomiting on their bed as I cried and tried to explain what I had done.

I spent three days in the ICU and was diagnosed with anorexia, depression, and anxiety by the time I graduated high school. Despite my willingness to get help and participate in treatment, my life continued to unravel. I went to therapy, tried multiple medications, and did a lot of soul-searching.

Meanwhile, I received an academic scholarship for college and graduated with a Bachelor of Science, majoring in psychology. I learned about borderline personality disorder during one of those courses and finally related to my chronic feelings of emptiness. A friend let me borrow a book called *I Hate You—Don't Leave Me* by Jerold J. Kreisman, MD and Hal Straus.

After an awful experience with a psychiatrist in 2018, I found a new primary care doctor who wanted to know why I was prescribed so many antidepressants. I explained that I had been treated for anxiety and depression, and was pretty sure I had borderline personality disorder. We went over my mental health history, and I explained my most frustrating daily life struggles. He pulled out a sheet of paper and asked me to take a test. After I finished, he took one look at the test and said, "See, you do not listen. I told you to only take the top section, but you took the whole thing."

He diagnosed me with attention deficit hyperactivity disorder (ADHD) and adjusted my medication. For the first time, at the age of thirty-five, I felt relief from the inner turmoil. I was also able to stop abusing other substances after realizing that the addictions and self-destructive behaviors stemmed from the untreated ADHD. I was trying to numb internal feelings of insecurity, shame, guilt, and emptiness. I needed to be able to block out intrusive thoughts and external noise, searching for peace from the constant chaos I felt.

I started researching and learned a lot of my feelings and odd behaviors were really common among neurodivergent people. I was happy to finally know the source of my inner turmoil but also frustrated at the thought of how my life could have been, if only I had been given the correct diagnosis and medication from my teens. You know what they say about hindsight.

These experiences of being let down by the mental health system led me toward a more empathetic way of viewing my personality. I started going to church again to feel closer to God and focused on my faith. I began listening to the voice in my heart, the one I felt was from God. Using what I had learned studying astrology, I began viewing myself through a spiritual lens. What the medical field saw as "pathological," I saw as patterns of behavior that just needed a little bit of balancing. It was easier to forgive myself this way.

When it came to love and relationships, I needed someone who understood the trauma I had been through. I needed someone who could handle my big emotions. In the past, I had tried to please everyone and often sacrificed my own needs just to avoid conflict. I didn't have any boundaries, and I had little self-esteem. An unplanned pregnancy at age twenty-one and losing my first love to a drug overdose at twenty-three was followed by the loss of many friends or family who either overdosed or committed suicide. A lot of self-sabotage, a few addictions, bankruptcy, and a divorce later, I fell in love again in 2016. I really lost myself during that relationship, and when it ended I felt like I had died once again. I stopped searching for happiness in someone else. I was never going to be able to love anyone until I loved myself.

I have a childlike soul that people often confuse with a refusal to grow up. But I don't see why I can't stay young at heart. My body will continue to age, and my mind will continue to gain wisdom, but my soul will remain as it always has been, no matter what age I am. I just think my internal view of life does not fit well into reality, or at least into society.

I find comfort in the lyrics of my muse, Taylor Swift. From her very first CD until now, she always had the perfect song, and the perfect lyric for every feeling I couldn't find words for. I've always thought she was a lyrical genius and an absolute mastermind. So many times, I have wanted to give her a hug, whether it was to say thank you for the perfect song for my heartbreak or because I saw and felt her pain every time the world was so cruel to her. I said to myself, *I don't know how she can handle all that hate from all over the world. I can't even take the heat from the small town I come from.*

I tend to have an all-or-nothing outlook on life and realized I needed to find more balance in multiple arenas. Beyond this healing music, I also sought out creatives, healers, and mediums. I listened to tarot card readings on YouTube to fall asleep at night. I found friends who are just as "crazy" as I am. Every new connection expanded my tribe of like-minded people and increased that sense of balance.

For me, the biggest and most profound part of my journey was choosing to share my story in this anthology. Two years ago, all the messages from that psychic medium immediately changed my direction. Her warning of suicide left me desperate to find a way to let go of all the pain I was carrying. I refused to let the cycle continue. When my health started declining about six months later, I realized that I had put myself on the bottom of the list again.

Reliving twenty years' worth of trauma during an already extremely stressful time in my life led me to crumble under the pressure, at least in the eyes of my loved ones. During an "intervention," they blamed my declining health on writing this chapter. I looked at them as if they were the "crazy" ones. This anthology has been the best thing I have ever been a part of.

I couldn't understand how they could blame my physical and mental health on something I didn't even begin writing until a few months ago. Yet I began questioning my own sanity, which proved I wasn't ready or strong enough to share my story. So I checked myself into the behavioral health unit they had found for me. I had been through so much; anyone would have been crushed under the pressure I had put on myself. I was willing to throw everything away that I worked so hard for. I was ready to blame everyone else for my inability to finish what I started.

Something changed once the door slammed and I was left with only myself to focus on. I realized that not only could I have said no and not admitted myself in the first place, but I could also still finish this chapter. I was the thirteenth patient to come in that night (my lucky number), and I met two young women, both named Grace. They reminded me of myself, and I realized that I can't quit just because things didn't go as planned. I used my time there to finish this final draft and to share my life lessons with these young women I met on the way to my final destination.

I am home now and feeling stronger than ever. Sometimes, I just need a reality check. No matter how hard it gets, I will never stop trying to be a better version of myself than I was the day before. If you want to know my secret, it is really quite simple. My magic potion consisted of faith, hope, and love … and a little bit of God's grace.

Amy Jones is a mother of two from Wood River, Illinois. She resides in Troy, Illinois, with her soulmate, Brad. A free spirit with a sensitive soul, she is passionate when it comes to love and Taylor Swift. After being diagnosed with "borderline lupus" last year, she left her job two weeks before a scheduled hysterectomy to focus on her physical and mental health. Amy hopes that by sharing her personal journey with mental health and addiction, she can help break the stigma and lead others to the path of self-love. Often described as the girl whose smile lights up every room she enters, she hopes to be a glimmer of hope to those still struggling. She believes that being vulnerable is courageous and that the antidote to shame is empathy.

Dr. Kristin Gaines Porlier

The Voice Inside

Have you ever felt anxiety without end? Ever felt like giving up on your dream? You are not alone.

In my twenties I was having fun in college and preparing for graduation. Among the first of my friends to get married, everyone expected us to start having babies right away. Slowly through my late twenties and early thirties my friends settled down, got married, and started having children.

I always knew I wanted kids, but I kept telling myself *I have time*. I wanted to graduate and start a big multidisciplinary practice first. Graduation came and went, and I opened a chiropractic office, not realizing how long it would take to build a business sufficient to provide for my family while paying off student loans. I worked seven days per week and attended business and coaching seminars to learn how to build an office. I struggled to grow and started to feel like a failure. I had spent all this time working hard in school and then working to grow my business, but the needed income wasn't coming in. Business coaches at seminars told me it would take five years to grow a business before you would really see a paycheck. Already feeling a little burnt out, I also felt my biological clock ticking, urging me to start my family.

After five years, my practice was successful enough to foster bigger dreams of owning a building that specialized in health and wellness options ... and I still desperately wanted to have a baby. The voice inside me told me to scale back on the dream of owning a building and start focusing on my family. I already owned my practice, and it was thriving, my husband had built a home, and we did some traveling, but we both felt something was still missing: children to share our lives with and give love to.

My husband and I were not prepared for the long journey we were about to embark on. Many people spend their younger adult years trying to prevent pregnancy, while I struggled to get pregnant. All my friends started having babies at the same time. I attended baby shower after baby shower, secretly wishing that one day it would be my turn to celebrate. The heartache of not having a child of my own started to weigh on me as I felt left out and alone. I did have freedom to travel with my husband, carefree and spontaneous, but I started to feel disconnected from friends. Their talk was about sleepless nights and changing disgusting diapers. I'd hear strangers in the store complain about how unruly their children were and their frustrations as parents.

Many comments directed to me, even in passing, were upsetting. I didn't want to share my feelings for fear of ruining others' happiness, and I also wanted to always look "put together." I am a perfectionist who knows I am not perfect but doesn't want others to see me struggling. Feeling so vulnerable and forever hiding it created a painful and shame-filled cycle. I became bitter to the point of not wanting to be around friends. My husband and I patiently waited for years until it was clearly time for some intervention.

As a chiropractor, I have been able to help many people with natural, non-pharma, and non-invasive supports on their fertility journey. Why was I struggling? I, too, embraced the holistic treatments of chiropractic, acupuncture, and nutrition that helped many couples in my practice balance their bodies better and achieve pregnancy.

After natural conception and holistic supports didn't result in pregnancy, I finally decided to visit a fertility specialist for the first steps of tests for me and my husband. Those found no significant reason why I was struggling to get pregnant, other than a condition I've had since my teen years, polycystic ovary syndrome. The doctor was confident that I could become pregnant. Telling no one outside our immediate family at first, I started the rigorous treatments to reach my dream of becoming a mother. I felt ashamed that my body was struggling to achieve pregnancy. We progressed to intrauterine insemination and additional testing.

Months of multiple IUIs and diagnostic procedures brought no success. The doctor then changed the medications that stimulate ovulation, and the new ones caused weight gain, debilitating anxiety, and crying spells.

Is this worth all the pain? I wondered. But the voice within was nagging me to move forward.

Finally, we tried implantation of a fertilized ovum. We were hopeful when they were able to harvest many eggs. After another year of trying medications and implantation, we were pregnant, and at my initial pregnancy exam everything looked great! A healthy heartbeat and my climbing levels of human chorionic gonadotropin (hCG) confirmed success.

At exactly seven weeks, my husband and I were out at a restaurant for breakfast when I began to bleed. I called the doctor immediately, but it was St. Patrick's Day and a weekend, so the office was closed. The on-call doctor told me to go home, rest, and stay hydrated, and wait to see if the bleeding would stop. It didn't. The flow began to increase, and I was having a lot of cramping and back pain.

The emergency room visit was ironically painful, as the nurse attending me was pregnant with twins. I waited an agonizing five hours for an ultrasound tech to confirm I had lost the baby. My heart was shattered, as were all the hormones in my body, creating a chemical cr*p storm of emotion. I was filled with sadness and awful anxiety.

The months required before we could try again passed, waiting for my body to be hormonally prepped for another round. A miscarriage elevates the hCG hormone associated with pregnancy for weeks before your level returns to zero. Once you have a menstrual cycle, you can begin the IVF process again. I lived with multiple daily injections, gaining weight, and feeling miserable again, while trying to hide all that from the world outside my home. But several months later, we became pregnant again!

As I approached my first ultrasound appointment, this time at six weeks, I started to get excited. We saw a heartbeat, and again the signs were hopeful; but a second checkup one week later revealed that the baby had stopped growing. My pregnancy became a wait-and-see game, and my mind raced with anxiety and fear. *Am I losing this pregnancy too? What is wrong? Why is this happening? Did I do something wrong?* I prayed multiple times daily that my baby would be OK.

Again, I started to bleed and lost the baby, this time on our wedding anniversary. Having another miscarriage made that anniversary a day shrouded in grief.

My husband, doctor, and I were still hopeful for success as we started round three of IVF and again reached a positive pregnancy test! After our prior losses, I could feel the fear setting in, but I tried to be optimistic. Soon it was time for my first ultrasound ... which revealed there was no baby. Heartbroken again, we learned about chemical pregnancy: a positive test but no fetus.

My fertility specialist discovered a small obstacle to be resolved before the next round of IVF. This obstacle would delay the IVF process another few months. But now this little voice in my head said *run more tests*. I knew there must be something causing me to lose these babies. When I shared my thoughts with the doctor, she assured me of the protocol and said, "You *have* been able to get pregnant, so let's stick with the protocol."

Soon, I was ready for round four, but something kept telling me I needed a change. I had heard of an innovative fertility specialist and decided to visit with her. Don't get me wrong: my specialist was amazing, and a caring nurse from one of my early docs moved on to the staff of this specialist, so she was with me for the whole journey. And another of my nurses became my friend and is still a part of my life today.

After yet another year of no success, my little brother and his wife had a baby, and all my friends had a few kids by now. I dreaded going to baby showers. A few friends found success with IVF on the first try, and although I was happy for them, I was also frustrated. I felt awful for being angry, but I bypassed social media and avoided hanging out with friends who had children. It was excruciating to not have one of my own.

Listening still to that voice within, I asked for more testing from that innovative specialist. A series of tests revealed no explanation for all my lost pregnancies. Genetic tests returned normal results for me and my husband. Even my three dozen harvested embryos were tested. The doctors called me an anomaly.

One test showed my natural killer cells were elevated, which indicated an overactive immune system. After treatment for that, I became pregnant once again. Our baby had a healthy heartbeat, and all other measures of my health and the baby's gave us hope for a successful pregnancy. At eight weeks I suffered another miscarriage.

My husband suggested adoption, and we visited a few agencies and chose one for application. The night before submitting it, that little voice within kept nagging me to try one last time. I told my husband, "I think

God is speaking to me and telling me to pursue IVF again." We elected to try one more time.

For the next round, I felt sure I needed two embryos "planted." I continued to pray daily, eat well, access chiropractic and acupuncture, and take my vitamins. Our doctors were unanimously against implanting two embryos, but that voice inside told me: *just do it*. Once again, we had success! I was terrified for those few weeks leading up to the first ultrasound. I prayed every time I sat down that I would not see blood when I stood.

One day I saw blood, and my heart sank. *Not again.* The ultrasound that day revealed a healthy heartbeat, but only one. The pregnancy continued, and I remained fearful that the worst would happen … but it didn't! I gave birth to a beautiful, healthy baby girl in 2021!

Sharing my story, while painful and vulnerable, made me realize I am not alone. Listening to that voice within and leaning on trusted family and friends gave me strength to keep dreaming, all these challenging years. Faith, trust, and prayer carried me through my darkest moments and into the light!

Sometimes in the face of big challenges, dreams may change. I never know what the future holds or where life will take me. But now I have become an advocate for myself. Now I will forever trust the voice within, follow its guidance, and keep stretching toward my dreams.

Dr. Kristin Gaines Porlier is a Christian, wife, and mother. She has a bachelor's degree in life science and a doctorate in chiropractic and functional medicine. She is an author, with internationally published articles in the field of chiropractic; a speaker; and she owns a family chiropractic practice in Missouri. Dr. Porlier has served as chiropractor for professional athletes and an Olympic medalist. She enjoys spending time out on the lake with her husband, daughter, and boxer dog. She is a competitive water skier and Guinness World Record holder in water skiing. After her own struggles, Dr. Porlier specializes in helping pregnant women as well as children, striving to find the root cause of her patients' health issues through chiropractic, acupuncture, and functional medicine.

April Imming

My Happily Ever After

"I never signed up for your disability!" my husband of twenty-four years screamed at me immediately after I found out about his affair. I could not believe what I was hearing. Did he believe my disability justified his betrayal of our marriage? Who was this monster standing before me? How could the man I'd loved for most of my life be so heartless?

I felt my heart being ripped out of my chest. He was my everything, my best friend, my lover, my person. His voice was the first thing I heard in the morning and the last thing I heard at night. And now he was leaving to live a new life; our relationship, our marriage, and our family were tossed out like yesterday's trash.

To tell my story, I need to start twenty-one years before this heartbreak. My husband and I, happily married for just two years and six months, owned a little lunch restaurant in Alton, Illinois. I ran the restaurant while my husband worked in the construction field. Though only recently married, our relationship already spanned almost a decade. With our son and his new baby sister, our family now numbered four. My story felt like a fairy tale. How could I know that a villain in the form of a disease was about to take center stage in our lives?

This thief in the night first stole my peace with excruciating headaches. Then one day the vision in my left eye went dark. After many tests by several doctors, my husband and I sat in a neurologist's office waiting to hear the latest results. The outlaw emerged and commanded attention with a name: multiple sclerosis. As the doctor explained the details of MS and the treatments available, the only words I heard were, "There is no cure."

I felt I'd been handed a death sentence with a very long stay of execution. Little by little, multiple sclerosis was going to steal my life from me as I watched, powerless to stop it. After the initial shock, and with the support from my husband, family, and friends, I became determined to *never* allow this disease to define who I am: MS is not me! I resolved never to complain about the constant pain. Unless you knew me well, you would not know I had MS.

Several years after my diagnosis, our family grew again with the birth of our youngest, and my husband took a new job out of state. This leap was an incredible sacrifice he made to provide for all of us because family meant everything to the man I married. The kids and I were his world, just as he was mine. We were all brokenhearted each time he left for this new work, knowing we wouldn't see him again for several weeks or months. Like all families, we had our struggles, but somehow we made it work … that is, until we didn't.

When he returned home, I saw signs of my husband changing. For as long as I can remember, he was a social butterfly, the life of the party, and the center of attention. Now he seemed to have moved beyond *wanting* attention to somehow needing it. But for me, coping with extreme fatigue as one of the primary symptoms of MS, keeping up with my husband's new craving for nightlife was difficult.

Soon his visits home were no longer spent with me and the kids but indulging in the evening entertainment our little town had to offer. Beyond my being unable to join his preferred activities, he seemed to now be blaming me for anything that went wrong in our lives. His visits home became punctuated with verbal abuse and toxic arguments.

The mistreatment was a huge red flag, and I should have grabbed the kids and run. Yet I honestly thought I could fix whatever evil he was going through. Unwilling to give up on the deep bond of our early marriage, I sincerely thought I had enough love in me to make him want to be a better person, a better father, a better husband. As I struggled to hold onto my marriage, the effects of MS suddenly became public: I was losing my ability to walk.

Life sometimes felt unbearable. I could not choose which was worse: struggling with the symptoms of MS, mistreatment by someone I loved, or missing the person I had vowed to spend the rest of my life with. But I no longer recognized in my husband that man I had married.

The kids no longer cried for their father; instead, they rejoiced whenever he left for work again. To them, life was happier when he wasn't around.

I tried so hard to make his world better, even prioritizing his demons over my health. I blamed myself for having a disability and for how it rendered me incapable of being the person he needed me to be. No matter what I corrected, I couldn't fix *me* … there is no cure for MS.

And then, finally, in our twenty-fourth year of marriage, came the infidelity. He didn't even try to hide it. He felt no guilt, no remorse, no shame.

Our last time together as a family is a day I wish I could forget. The anger in his eyes cut right through my heart. Why was he angry at me? He is the one who had the affair!

Though the foundation of all we'd built had begun crumbling more than ten years before, on this day the walls collapsed and the roof caved in. I felt I was watching our life, our family, our love burning to the ground with no fire truck in sight. My story would not end with a *happily ever after*. And then he was gone, and the kids and I were left to sift through ashes and gather any lightly charred timbers we could to construct a temporary shelter. Our story was on pause until I figured out what the next chapter would look like.

Depression settled upon me like the weight of the world. There were mountains of rocky pain on my shoulders, and my tears were endless rivers filling my soul with a dark lake of grief and despair. The weight of the boulders crushing my chest caused every breath to labor, and the thorny vines cluttering my path cut deep into my heart no matter what move I made. Multiple sclerosis became a walk in the park compared to the depression kicking my a**! I honestly thought I might die from a broken heart.

And just when I thought I couldn't bear another tragic moment, a mammoth-sized bulldozer arrived to remove the remaining ashes of my Once Upon a Time. My children and I all received a group text message from his mistress. In the first few sentences, she called me a wh*r*. The woman having an affair with my husband, in a text to our children and me, called me a vulgar name for a harlot. She made fun of my disability and the difficulties I have standing. She was not writing to apologize for the torment she and my husband had caused our family. She was not making amends for the part she took in my husband abandoning our family. She had no issues with the father of my children choosing her over them.

My mind filled with questions: How did she know the details of my pain? Together, were they laughing about my struggles with MS? Why would anyone make fun of someone with a disability?

The pain of continued, expanded depression was excruciating. How would I muster up the energy to move on? Turning fifty and on disability, my twenty-four-year marriage over, and the father of my children with another family. I was angry and sad. I wanted to scream. I wanted to know *why*. I was losing myself. Depression and MS were working together to finish the destruction of my life, my family, and my Once Upon a Time.

However, I could not declare surrender, for in the middle of all the gloom and despair were my children. I needed to pick myself up from this rock bottom because I could see my pain adding to what my children already felt. After all, he didn't just leave me. He walked away from them too. He built a whole new world without *them* in it. As hard as it might be, I needed to build a new world for my children, one without mistreatment, judgment, and constant arguments. A world full of love and honesty. They deserved happiness more than he did.

So, like a phoenix rising from the ashes, I took the lead in a new family fairy tale. Sure, MS will always be the dragon lurking from its lair in my new story, and from time to time the rogues of my ex and his girlfriend rear their ugly heads. But with the support of my children, family, and friends, we slowly moved to our new normal.

No days are easy, and many days reveal a new burned-out room, in which case we must remodel. I needed time to mourn and let go of the person I married because it seems that person is long gone. I had to learn to love myself again, and, yes, love the girl with MS. A dear friend reminds me that multiple sclerosis isn't who I am but what makes me strong.

Now I know that not having a cure for MS was never the problem. The problem was not surrounding myself with strong, honest, amazing people. People who choose to lift each other up. My kids and I had to adjust to being a one-parent family, and we leaned on each other for love and support.

I see no possibility in my future timeline when the pain goes away or when the tears stop. When I'm sad, I let myself be sad. If I need to cry, I grab the best pint of ice cream and I cry. For a long time, I thought of my love story as a tragic one, a love lost. I now see a love was found: my love for myself.

And now I have some great knights guarding our fairy tale kingdom. My castle may have burnt to the ground from an assault by a distant catapult named *mistress*, but we will rebuild our Camelot to be greater and stronger than the first. This traumatic chapter in our story has built incredibly strong bonds among me and my children. These bonds are so strong, not even Excalibur could break them. I will always be a hopeless romantic, and in this new fairytale, my happily ever after is my strong, loving, and loyal children.

April Imming is a devoted mother of three who has spent a majority of her life working with children and adults who live with physical and mental disabilities. She also assisted high school students in a national engineering competition addressing workplace barriers for people with disabilities. Two teams competed in Washington, D.C., and both placed in the top five.

April continues as an educator about people living with MS and other disabilities, and plans to expand the telling of her story with the publication of her memoir. In her spare time, she loves to read or create adventures with her beloved pets, and enjoys nights out with friends, visits to local museums, and scavenging in local shops for antiques.

Her best moments are spent just listening to her children laugh.

Nancy Ortinau

Seeds of Resilience: Cultivating Healing and Growth

The loss of loved ones—too many, too close together—once imprisoned me behind a veil of grief so dark that I couldn't envision my future. I felt trapped in a fragile bubble, adrift in an immense realm of uncertainty, unable to find direction or purpose as I wandered, my eyes clouded with sorrow.

My life inside that world of grief became an unsettling ride of highs and lows. Losing my younger brother "Doug" suddenly in an unfathomable accident was a surreal twist that left me scrambling for answers. Thoughts of his wife and his children, still so innocent and untouched by life's harsh realities, only added to the overwhelming sense of injustice. "I just cannot believe this happened to him. Why him? Why now?" Many unanswered questions echoed through me, and I felt trapped in a waking nightmare I could not reconcile with the world as I once knew it.

At family gatherings, Doug was the spotlight of humor and warmth. He had quick wit, and his infectious laughter radiated through the room, earning him the title of the family's comedian. My adult bond with this closest sibling among the eight of us matured into something truly special, sharing childhood memories, adult aspirations, and dreams that became a treasure chest of remembered conversations. Doug became my mentor and biggest cheerleader for my roles as a mom and business entrepreneur.

When our older brother came to live with my husband and me due to his illness, we faced difficult decisions regarding his care and well-being. Having Doug by my side provided an invaluable source of support. Each conversation with him filled me with strength and understanding.

Exactly four years following Doug's death, "Kate," my dear friend of more than thirty years, succumbed to complications after a surgery. She passed away in the same hospital room Doug did, during the same week of the year. Kate was more than a friend; she was a sister to me. We were joined at the hip, as sisters should be, and even married men with the same name! Our children, close in age, made outings extra special. Kate and I shared an unbreakable bond, and her loss felt unbearable, especially after losing Doug. Losing these two loved ones, who knew me better than I knew myself, was profound, like losing big pieces of my heart.

This double anniversary of loss is of particular significance every year, as it is the same week as my birthday. My dear friend and my brother had never failed to offer me those cherished birthday wishes one deserves on their special day.

My grief deepened as my older brother fell gravely ill and passed away one year later. Three short years after that, our youngest brother also left us. Four deaths in my closest family in eight years joined additional losses during these years—aunts, uncles, and godparents— and turned me into a stoic person, unable to function. I felt a profound sense of disorientation, constantly haunted by the questions: *What comes next? Who comes next?* With only five of us remaining in our sibling group, the fear of who I might be mourning next consumed my mind for weeks.

My precious husband walked with me along this trail of death, and we both struggled to make sense of so much loss. I felt these losses deeply, especially not being able to pick up the phone and talk with that special person. Life was just not the same. How does one find new friends and family? My husband tried to become that go-to support person as I withdrew further and further into myself. Approaching retirement, he was working so much that our time together was severely limited. He has been my pillar of strength since we met as teenagers, and watching me suffer was heartbreaking for him.

So, mostly coping alone with my grief during the pandemic quarantines, I embarked on a journey for inner peace. I turned to gardening: tending my flower beds, creating new ones, and cherishing the tranquility, peace, and quiet of the outdoors. My husband's unique work schedule during this period provided time for us to also build a vegetable garden. Preparing the garden, planting the seeds, and watching the plants grow was exciting.

To our dismay, the appetites of deer, rabbits, and squirrels were well satiated by the fruits of our labor. By season's end, we decided to venture into vertical gardening. As a health and wellness coach at the time, I thought it made total sense to start this new vertical gardening journey. With eager anticipation, we started our new gardening journey in our basement.

"What an amazing way to grow vegetables," I exclaimed to my friend over coffee. "You wouldn't believe how fast they grow." Pausing, he thoughtfully replied, "Why not share what you are doing at my networking meeting on Friday?" I pondered stepping out of my comfort zone and speaking in front of everyone. "I don't know if I could do that." My friend reassured me, "Just come and see."

All of a sudden it was Friday, and I was determined to honor my commitment. "I promised I would come, so I will!" Walking into the meeting, I encountered fellow business owners full of energy and enthusiasm. Recognizing some familiar faces was reassuring. Sharing my garden experience proved challenging, but I persevered. As I left, a sense of rejuvenation washed over me. Already embarking on new friendships,

I was also launching a new gardening business. Anticipation for the next Friday opportunity bubbled inside me.

Today a new person has been born within me. Excitement and vitality flow through my body, and hope fills me. I am on the path to overcoming this grief, with a newfound sense of determination to get more active again after the long months indoors, reclaiming fitness and energy. This new adventure provides focus, and people are genuinely interested in what I have to say.

I no longer hide behind my struggles with lack of confidence or fear of making mistakes. Instead I am driven to encourage others to find a healthy new life through food and nutrition. My husband and I strive to find new friends and share close bonds every day, which has given us a clear sense of purpose.

Looking back with today's wisdom and hindsight, I can see that my stoicism began much earlier than this series of deaths, stemming from experiences with my father in my early years. Raised in an era of inequality, the abundance of perfectionism and control my father brought to the family dynamics was life altering and mentally damaging. As a young girl, I learned I needed to embody the idea of a perfect submissive female, both mentally and physically. Enduring physical abuse and witnessing his uncontrolled anger as a teenager, the memory of his fist still haunts me. The last time he pummeled my tender teenage body, the emotional pain finally topped the physical pain. From that day forward, I vowed never to allow anyone to terrify me again. I learned to be tough as nails and assumed what would remain my stoic stance in life. But under my *I've Got This* exterior, I always harbored a desire to again trust in sharing my life with others.

Just as my healing was underway, my husband's retirement loomed on the horizon, providing me the great opportunity to trust in this new way. After dedicating himself to a job for forty-five years, often working sixty or more hours per week, he came home without a concrete plan for this next chapter of life. After a couple of years of wandering through days with no set routine, he decided to join me in my endeavors. Witnessing the passion reignited inside me, he suggested expanding my business. "We need to do this together," he said, "to teach others how to do what you are doing." And I watched with delight as *his* passion came to life. The excitement bubbling inside of me was like a child in a candy store choosing her favorite piece of chocolate.

As I write this story, the grand opening of Nancy's Urban Tower Farm is just around the corner. We are scurrying to get all the pieces in place to reveal our amazing aeroponic tower farm. We are thrilled to share our pleasure, teach the importance of growing one's own food for higher nutritional value, and help others learn new methods of farming both indoors and outdoors. We look forward to the immense pleasure of witnessing children's joy as they experience this wonderful horticulture during field trips. We can't wait to see their sweet faces filled with excitement. Additionally, we look forward to busloads of residents from senior centers spending time with us, enjoying access to gardening again.

Although it has taken me sixty-five years to find my life's passion, I love working alongside my husband every day. We are the dynamic duo, having found each other anew, like the last puzzle piece for completion. Now is my time to teach and help other women attain their goals, despite their struggles, and through the revelations they bring to never give up on their true desires. My heartwarming journey today includes the satisfaction of passing the torch of knowledge, gratitude, and inspiration to women seeking success in their endeavors. To trust others wholeheartedly, allowing them to perceive the authentic individual I embody, is the burning desire I harbored deeply inside, which is now finally realized. My heart is overflowing with joy and excitement as I watch others begin their journeys.

Nancy Ortinau, owner of Nancy's Urban Tower Farm, LLC and Inspirations by Nancy, LLC, is an expert in growing on vertical gardening systems. On her live broadcast, *Cooking with Nancy O*, she shares recipes to help others eat healthier using simple steps of cooking, and her *Inspirations by Nancy* podcast shares healthy living habits. Nancy's passion is to build tower farms all over the world. She was educated in "Garden of Your Dreams" and "Garden of Your Dreams Worldwide," by Matthieu Mehuys in Belgium.

Michelle Huelsman

A Farewell's Echo

Many things we never remember. A few things we can never forget. I remember this moment like it was yesterday.

It's dusk. A ray of sunlight ever so slightly illuminates the bed in our Denver, Colorado, hotel room. My father is lying down covered up, and the room is quiet. My stepmom is trying to fade into the walls as the moment has come for me to say goodbye. I lean against the bed; my hand is on my dad's as he pats my cheek. We gaze at each other for a few moments as the clock on the nightstand ticks. Finally, I can't take the silence anymore and start to move away. My dad grabs my hand to stop me, then whispers his final words to me, "I am so sorry. I love you, and I know you will be OK."

It's fall of 2017, and I am driving home from work when I receive the call from my dad that he has been having trouble with his left arm and is not sure what's going on. He has an appointment with the doctor in a couple days because he's been "off" ever since he got a flu shot. I have a gut feeling and make a mental note of how strange this seems. I ultimately conclude he probably just pulled a muscle, as carpenters regularly do.

Throughout the winter holidays, my daily two-minute conversations with my dad continue while the mental note keeps creeping in. I begin to wonder, *What ever happened with Dad's arm? Did the doctors discover anything?* Caught up in my own life, I begin to realize we haven't talked about the subject again.

Once the holidays wrap up, January brings the news of Dad having to see a specialist because his arm is growing weaker. Local doctors in the small town of Steamboat can't make a diagnosis, so they are sending him to Denver. His appointment is next week, and I'm not to worry. Not to worry? I mean … like how do I not? The news is a shocker; whatever is wrong, is it something worse than what basic testing reveals?

The next week of work is filled with chaos. Then Dad calls with the results of his appointment, and time stops. Work chaos no longer matters; my job, the employees I manage, and customers don't matter. The doctors think he has Guillain-Barre syndrome (GBS), which can result from a vaccine. This news triggers the memory of when his arm first started hurting and that small connection I had made but brushed away. But to be sure it's Guillain-Barre, he needs more testing and requires frequent trips to the doctor over the next few months.

The thousand miles between us is all I can think about. The distance, the diagnosis, the journey he is going through without my help is earth shattering and *so* terrifying. This man who is my rock, biggest supporter, pillar of strength, idol, basically the world, my dad is in trouble and there is nothing I can do but wait.

As winter becomes spring, we continue our two-minute daily check-ins, but during each call I feel something is being hidden. So I pack a bag, hop on a plane, and head to Steamboat. When I pull into the driveway and see him for the first time in a year, I am blown away. He is still tall, strong, and has his wits about him, but his left arm is half the size of his right. There is no muscle mass, and it dangles at his side like a leaf in the wind.

I learn he has been prescribed a round of intravenous immunoglobulin (IVIG). This treatment made from donated blood contains healthy antibodies that fight against and dilute the Guillain-Barre antibodies, which cause nerve damage. The IVIG eases symptoms and shortens GBS duration. Dad explains the process, what the doctors say about it, and shows me pictures of the different types of medicine he will be given. Talk about a *hard* conversation! Once again, he mentions the doctors are not 100 percent certain GBS is the correct diagnosis.

I travel home feeling just as confused and fearful as when I set out for Steamboat. Partial answers aren't really answers. I return home full of questions, not fully understanding what is happening. Having no say in the medical decisions, I feel alone as I navigate through this new leg of Dad's journey.

My husband and a couple of close friends try to listen and understand, but few in my circles know I have a sick parent. Work demands are rising, and I realize I am drowning. I am physically and mentally drained, and time is now moving fast … too fast. I hold tough conversations with Dad and other family members about lawyers, paperwork, and wills being drawn.

During the last week of April, my dad has his treatment. Our fingers and toes are crossed, but as spring heats up to summer it is clear that GBS is not the final diagnosis. His weight keeps declining, he is having trouble eating and walking. New symptoms are developing quickly.

Finally, I get The Call. Dad is diagnosed with Lou Gehrig's disease. I cannot wrap my brain around what this means. What is happening? Why? Surely, there must be a way to fix my dad! What do you mean he might not exist in six months?!

In this moment of pure anguish and despair, I know in my gut that I need help, mentally and physically. I must process and deal with how this is hitting *me*. I realize my body is also trying to deal with stress, as

I face the possibility of losing my father. Mentally and emotionally, I am equally tired and sore, and my heart always hurts. I do not want to become someone full of hate or sadness. So I grab my phone and ask friends and family for referrals to a grief therapist.

I now can see this desperate grab for sanity as the most life-changing turn in my life's road.

My grief therapist and I meet every other week until July when it is clear that Dad's treatments are not working. The doctors are out of suggestions. My dad is struggling. Unable to swallow, not interested in eating or drinking, he cannot use his left arm at all, and he is having trouble walking and sleeping. Now the harsh realities we had been facing for months become more jagged and painful for the whole family. Life's limit feels right around the corner.

I increase my time from biweekly to weekly sessions with the grief therapist. My family dynamics pour into our sessions. Narcissistic traits of one family member, my parents' divorce, abuse … all rolled out like a thread off a spool. The therapist uses eye movement desensitization and reprocessing therapy (EMDR) to help me reach pieces of my past hidden behind closed doors in my mind. Memories full of anger, tears, heartache, and loneliness return from the past.

I never thought of myself as someone who needed therapy. I am not crazy, after all. But it turns out this opportunity to speak my truth to a neutral listener is exactly what I most need in my life but didn't know I needed. The visits allow me to process the loss I am now facing while allowing light into *all* the dark places. Therapy is a safe space where I cry and give words to whatever needs them, while also physically and mentally preparing myself for the worst to come.

That October, Dad's health declines so much that he needs a feeding tube. I just cannot believe it. My stepmom and I seize the opportunity to take Dad on a literal trip of a lifetime to Yellowstone National Park. I drive from Steamboat to Yellowstone with him in the back seat. He stares out the windows for hours, just contemplating, existing. I watch him watching the world move by—a world he is no longer able to fully grasp by its hands.

We are all subdued, tears running, conversations of the future and past spoken softly while the scenery of the West passes by. I feel deeply grateful for my hours with the grief therapist. I am mentally prepared, know how to handle tough conversations, can feel my feelings, name them, process them ... all the while staying present in these last moments of our lives together. He's grown so thin, so fast, and is barely able to sit in a car. But he is not going to let that get in the way. We drive all over Yellowstone and see elk, moose, bear, and wolves. It is so amazing, and the quality time spent in the car is priceless.

A few days later, I make my way back to our hotel room in Denver, tears streaming down my face uncontrollably, knowing that tomorrow morning I'll be flying back to St. Louis. Settling into our hotel room, the dimming light of the dusk softly illuminates the bed where my father lies covered up, and silence envelops the room. My stepmom fades into the background as the moment to bid farewell approaches. My father reassured me months/years ago that I would be OK, and I am. I've done the deep inner work, made peace, and said all that needed to be said.

This poignant moment is forever etched in my memory. Boarding the plane, returning home, resuming work, I learned that my father survived his surgery, only to succumb a few days later. His life, his words, his touch are no longer held by just a few breaths, but are now a farewell's echo.

My dad's end-of-life journey taught me how to grieve and the importance of self-care. Seeking support is crucial when challenged by grief and loss. But beyond coping with grief, I learned that it's OK to feel and express my emotions, even when they're raw and difficult. I learned that seeking help, whether from trusted friends, family, or professionals, can provide the support necessary to navigate dark times. Ultimately, this whole growth passage of my life turned out to be about emerging stronger, maintaining my sense of self, and knowing that it's OK to not be OK. Now I will always know that in my darkest moments, there is a path toward healing and resilience. I just need to be willing to discover it.

Michelle Huelsman | A Farewell's Echo

Michelle Huelsman earned a bachelor's degree in business from Lindenwood University in St. Charles, Missouri, and embarked on a career path that reflects her diverse passions and unwavering dedication. After more than fourteen years as a general manager in the restaurant industry, Michelle found her true calling in 2022 when she established herself as a professional photographer with her company, Unbridled Focus. Michelle's photography style is deeply influenced by her extensive experience working with people and her profound love for animals. In her free time, Michelle can be found riding, hanging out in a barn, or dedicating herself to volunteer work, all with crazy hair. Alongside her husband of eighteen years, Michelle enjoys traveling and cherishing moments with her two golden retrievers.

Abiegayle Winingar

Where Is My Respect?!

This feeling of a smack in the face with a two-by-four was very apparent as I stared at the ten words on my page. Suddenly, I was reviewing every relationship of my twenty-nine years of life and seeing something I had not noticed before. At some point, I had lost my self-respect and started allowing others to disrespect me. If you've shared this kind of sudden, unexpected insight into a painful pattern, you may have wondered, as I did, *Where did this start?*

In Part Two of training for practitioners of Neuro Linguistic Programming (NLP), I had just completed an exercise to define what I value in relationships. During this exercise, we listed values we deemed important in a topic we choose and then narrowed it down to our top ten. At first looking at my list, I thought *There's nothing wrong with it.* Then our coach looked at one of my classmates and asked, "What's missing in your list?" I immediately knew what was missing from her list, so I looked down at mine because ... well, what was missing from mine? That's when the two-by-four struck. Where was respect? I had said respect at least fifteen times during the exercise and yet it landed nowhere near my top ten.

Thinking back to discover when respect first sank in my priorities, I started with the very beginning: my biological father, aka The Sperm Donor. From the moment I was born, it seemed I was chasing affection from a man who could not care less whether I was alive. That may sound harsh, but he did tell me he didn't believe I was his and demanded a paternity test.

By the time I was five, I had a very clear understanding of feeling unwanted. One weekend my mom sent me to the car, and I lasted all of five minutes before returning for my first lesson in eavesdropping: if you don't want to hear it, then don't listen in. Even through the front door, I could hear my parents screaming at each other. My mom shouting, "It's only weekends; she's your kid too." And my father retorting, "You just want to drop her off to go do whatever you want." I thought if I behaved well enough or if I acted more boyish—masculine, like him—then he'd want me around more. Later, after years of his rejection and always feeling sure I did something wrong, I questioned my mom with tears streaming down my face, "Why doesn't he love me?" or "What did I do?"

Then, miraculously, after weeks or months of no visitation, I would be at his house for the weekend again. I learned if I drew enough attention by joking around, wanting to watch R-rated movies or to play more mature games such as *Grand Theft Auto*, then I would get small scraps of positive attention in return. That pattern of following along with what others enjoyed stayed with me into adulthood.

I told my mom one day in middle school that I did not want to see my father anymore. Then I returned to wanting contact with my father again a few years later. I realized that I had cut him out of my life quickly. I discovered I still missed him, though, and continued trying to rekindle a relationship off and on until my senior year of high school, when my newest attempt was to invite him to my graduation.

That bit me in the *ss when he used the invitation as a weapon against my mother in court, in an effort to stop paying child support. I hadn't realized that the location of the high school would reveal that I was living with my aunt rather than my mom. At that point, I cut complete contact with him and have not looked back. Finally, I stopped seeking attention from someone who could not give it.

My uncle was a second figure in my life who contributed significantly to my belief that I was worthless. At first, I was "his baby" in my early years. Mom, my aunt, and Nana all told me I was his favorite, out of everyone in my family (except Nana, who was his number one favorite). How quickly that changed when my cousin, his first son, was born.

Now that I have a child of my own, I understand that the relationship with your own child is just different. But my six-year-old mind couldn't wrap itself around the change in how he treated me. Someone who paid me attention every day suddenly walked away. I did everything I could: learned to fish and to shoot, and did my best in school. I thought if I excelled and made myself more like a son, then his attention would focus back on me. But it never worked; his son had replaced me.

My first long relationship was a ten-year, on-and-off-again cluster f*ck. That is honestly the best description. I chased his attention like it was candy and I could not get enough. He love-bombed me left and right, then ghosted me for days or weeks. He lied, and when I found out, he gaslit me so hard I could have started a fire. He cheated on me twice before learning to avoid my confronting him … *and* his "side gigs." His work-around to avoid fighting about his affairs was to first break up with me, start dating someone else without telling me, then cheat on and break up with *her*, to then come back to me. He was having his cake and eating it too.

Yet I loved him with all my heart and held him on a pedestal, believing he was the only one who really knew me. Early lessons of rejection had taught me that this disrespect was all I deserved. Life had taught me to stay silent in the face of dismissal by those who claimed to love me.

I suffered through ten years of this pattern, losing close friends and my mental health, all in the name of love, before I told myself that enough was enough.

Admitting not only on paper but in publication that "enough" was apparently *not* enough feels shameful, as if I really *am* deficient in some way. But I can't deny that even my most recent relationship, two years after that decade of pain, followed the same pattern. Simultaneously love-bombed and gaslit with "I love you, but it's OK if you don't say it. I know you don't love me as much as I do you." Once again I was chasing a love I craved, attempting to fill a void created so young, and allowing disrespect again and again. Finally, five months pregnant, I started pointing out the father's disrespect. I demanded better from the man who would help me raise our child.

When he threatened to take his own life and mine, I finally reached the end of my tolerance. This time it *really* was enough. I would not stand idly by and let someone else disrespect me. I had to respect myself enough to say, *This is not OK, and I am done. I deserve better.* Was being a single mother a scary thought? Yes, a little. However, I knew I could do it; my own mom was a good teacher.

When I stared at that NLP class list of my top ten values in relationships and noticed that respect was missing, it opened a door for a bigger change. I had to tear down those beliefs I had been building for decades. Having respect for myself meant I must stand up for my boundaries and let people know when they step on one, rather than allowing them to walk over my limits as if they are not even there. I started out slowly by not responding to people I saw as fighting against my limits. I distanced myself from them as my boundaries grew stronger. I voiced more boundaries, spoke up when someone acted as if they were an exception, and eventually cut some people off entirely.

I wish I had all along respected myself enough to speak when I was unhappy or wanted a change. I should have respected myself enough when my ex-boyfriend played his back-and-forth game. I wish I had said, "No. We broke up, so we are done, and I do not want to play this game." I wish I had respected myself enough to walk away or say something at the first red flag waved by my baby's father.

What I didn't know then but know now is that when I do not respect myself, I cannot expect others to respect me. Now I have truly learned what respect means to me.

Since I became certified in NLP, I have changed jobs to one where management has my back and the pay values my worth. I have stepped out of my comfort zone to write this chapter, sharing a painful piece of me with strangers. And I have grown my self-respect, which, in turn, has expanded the love I have for myself.

Now I live a life that shows my child what respecting yourself can do. He will witness me as I stand up for myself, as I recently did at work, telling my assistant manager, "I will not be doing that" when asked to break a rule. Before my training in NLP, I would have nodded my head and done what she requested, due to lack of self-respect. The question in the title of my chapter, "Where is my respect?" has taken me close to three decades to answer. The answer, of course, was inside me all along, just waiting until I was ready to receive it.

Abiegayle Winingar | Where Is My Respect?!

Abiegayle Winingar was born in Columbia, Missouri, and raised between there and St. Louis. She is proud mother to one beautiful dog named Theodore (Theo), who will be four in April, and one beautiful baby boy, who will be three in November. She holds a license in cosmetology and esthetics, and loves to use her knowledge to help those who struggle with their beauty routines. She also holds a certification in body sculpting and earned a Master Makeup Certificate. Abiegayle loves to read and has always wanted to publish, so this anthology made that dream come true. Her next dream is to create her own skin care line. She also loves DIY and art projects when she is not working. She is constantly learning new things and is a lover of history, the paranormal, and Halloween. Abiegayle hopes that her chapter inspires others to see in themselves what is there, waiting to be seen.

Helen Black

"I Am Here for You," He Said

I am number ten of fifteen kids. We grew up with our parents in a three-bedroom house in St. Louis, Missouri. Space was limited and we didn't get much attention, but we knew we were loved. Mom kept us in line while Dad worked. For several reasons, my siblings and I didn't have many friends growing up, but we had each other.

One wintry night when I was seventeen, a new friend introduced me to Rick. He was outgoing and had a lot of friends. His girlfriend had just broken up with him. My friend said, "He really likes you and would love to take you out on a date." I was single, so I accepted.

I didn't know anything about sex and boundaries or how to say "no." Soon I was pregnant. I didn't tell anyone, but Mom seemed to know. She told me if I continued the pregnancy, I would have to move out, So I left.

Rick convinced me to marry him by promising insurance coverage for the pregnancy and delivery. I wasn't thrilled with the idea because we hardly knew each other. But I agreed, and we were married just three months after our first date.

At that age, alcohol was something new in my life. Rick was one of the smartest guys I knew when he wasn't drinking. But he played in a band, and they drank heavily during practices. Fantasizing they'd be big rock stars someday, Rick quit his job to pursue this pipe dream, which terminated our medical insurance. Less than a year later, our firstborn arrived. We lived on unemployment in a one-bedroom apartment in St. Charles, Missouri, and I started working at a restaurant within walking distance.

Before our daughter was three months old, I became pregnant with baby number two. Rick was thrilled to learn we were having another baby, but I was the one working full time while pregnant and paying all the bills, while Rick and his band practiced daily, pulling in only a few low-paying gigs.

Our son was born when his big sister was just shy of thirteen months old. Rick seemed happy yet had recently started to treat me differently. He left us for days at a time, his drinking out of control, and he became physically abusive. One day, my sister who watched the kids while I worked called to say Rick was next door with a young female. I rushed home and found him drinking and playing guitar for her. He threw his drink in my face as soon as he saw me and began yelling that our son was not his, which wasn't true.

The abuse toward me escalated. Some days I went to work with a busted lip or a black eye. I no longer loved him, and his cheating made the idea of leaving seem easier. However, I had nowhere to go and didn't think I could make it as a single parent, so I started studying for my GED.

One night, I decided to go out with my neighbor, another mom. Rick dragged me right back into the apartment and beat the sh*t out of me, threatening me with a knife. Every time I tried to break away, Rick would come after me. I started blaming myself.

Then one night, Rick came home late wanting sex. I allowed it, to avoid his rage, and that led to my third pregnancy. This time, Rick threatened to leave me if I had the baby, and I thought, *well, if that's the case, I'll definitely keep the baby.*

Relatives started to see what was happening, but when they called him out, he came after me. This was the beginning of the end.

I decided to start making payments on a car at a used car lot without Rick knowing, but I didn't know how to drive. Baby number three, our second son, entered the world. I had to return to work after less than a week.

Finally, a tax return paid off the car and gave me a down payment for a mobile home. I persuaded Rick to teach me to drive so he wouldn't have to take me everywhere.

A friend helped me find a better-paying job. I made more money in one day than in a week of waitressing.

When our trailer and our land were ravaged by a Mississippi River flood, we moved in with my sister and her family. The $4,000 I'd saved to leave Rick went to help with living expenses. Yet I began to see how God was leading me, step by step, and I continually prayed for His plan to be revealed.

I was so tired. Treated horribly by customers all day, I came home to be treated worse by my husband. One day, I forgot my purse at work, holding the new stash of money I'd begun to save. My boss assured me she would keep it safe, but she stole it.

Completely fed up with the abuse, I told God I wished Rick was dead. Instead, I was in a horrible accident with an eighteen-wheeler. My car was totaled, but God made sure I walked away with only a couple stitches on the back of my head.

I had come so close to death that it was no longer my greatest fear. I started to stand up even more for myself and my three children. One day I came home to find Rick and his buddies in the basement, drinking and smoking pot. One of Rick's friends was being mean to our oldest boy, and I asked him not to talk to him that way. But Rick defended his friend.

After his friends left, Rick came to my room in a rage. I finally told him I didn't love him and couldn't live like this anymore. After pushing the dresser over in a crash, with a crazy look in his eyes, he began choking me. He broke away and left the room, but then my younger sister who was living with us came running down the hall.

"Leave!" she cried. "Get out of this house right now. Rick went downstairs to get his gun. Just take the car and go."

"But what about you and the kids?" I asked.

"He's not after us. He's after you." Handing me my keys, she continued, "Just leave. I don't care where you go, but you have to get out of here now."

Driving away was the greatest feeling I'd ever experienced. I knew this was it; I had finally broken away. *Where do I go now?* I knew I would never go back to that life again and that God had the steering wheel from this point on.

I came back home feeling God's presence all around me—scared but no longer afraid to die. I reasoned with Rick that if there was any chance for us, he would give me space and move out. I took the blame for our problems, told him I needed to learn who I was, and reminded him of how little personal space I grew up with. Rick agreed to allow me some time and space.

Nevertheless, he invaded our space by sneaking in one night. That was when I filed for a legal separation. But he didn't give up, showing up at his parents' home for Christmas Day. I let him spend alone time with the kids while I took a nap but then woke up with him, drunk and in my face, begging for another chance. When I said no, he started choking me and spit in my face. After his parents and brother intervened, I took the kids and left. We drove around looking at Christmas lights as I prayed to God for guidance.

Finally, the next spring, FEMA called to say they'd settled on my claims from the flood, for more than $20,000. Rick demanded half, and I relented to avoid a fight. My half went toward a house for the kids and me. But even this final separation of our lives wasn't smooth. While moving the appliances for me, one of his friends remarked how stupid Rick was for losing his kids and me, starting a huge fight between them.

I started to leave, then thought, *Wait a minute, this is my house; they need to leave.* While ushering everyone out, I found Rick in the basement. He then begged for another chance, and when I said no, he began choking me, then threw his bottle of alcohol across two rooms, knocking a hole in the wall. That's when I obtained a restraining order against him and filed for divorce. Again, it was God who provided strength and courage for those steps.

Rick didn't appear in court when the divorce became final, and I asked the judge for $200 per month for child support. The judge thought I could get more and assured me Rick could be locked up if he didn't pay it. I asked the judge whether he would be there to save me when Rick got out and came to kill me. I thank God for those perfect words.

I continued to cope with Rick's unstable emotions over the next twenty years. He created chaos for our adult kids and tried to hurt me with cruel words, but they no longer affected me.

Finally, Rick found God, stopped being so mean, and started paying child support. I couldn't believe it! He'd been in a homeless shelter in Las Vegas for a bit, then found a job and a place to live, and purchased a moped. He was saving money and studying to become a minister. God works in mysterious ways.

Not long after this news, I received a phone call from Rick's best friend to tell me that Rick had been killed in a hit-and-run. No one in Las Vegas would claim his body, so I claimed it and started a GoFundMe to help bring him home. He was laid to rest in the same cemetery with his family.

Through all those painful and chaotic years, God repeatedly proved to me that He is by my side always, through my darkest hours *and* my brightest days. He whispered in my ear and guided me in right directions.

I didn't always understand or listen, but I learned from my mistakes. He has given me a good life, and now I can see that, even during the hard days, I grew stronger and wiser. Having learned to lean on God, I now teach my grandchildren to ask for His guidance often.

As I look back on my life, the choices I made at a young age, and the tests God gave me, I feel proud of who I am today. I stopped asking God "Why me?" and started listening to His guidance. I recall God whispering into my ears, "Helen, I am here for you. I never left you. You, Helen, need to be there for yourself." His words brought me to my knees in tears because I knew He was right. I just needed to stop, listen, and learn.

And what I heard, what I learned, is that I am better than the pain I was in, and stronger than I realized. Once my deepest fears were behind me, particularly the fear of death, I learned I could heal and thrive with the support of my own personal Protector.

With God's love and protection, Helen Black survived a childhood of poverty and a marriage full of violence, overcoming it all to thrive. Now married to the love of her life for almost twenty years, she enjoys her administrative position at a university in St. Louis. Her three children, all born before she turned twenty-two, plus three bonus children who joined the family when she married her second husband, have now blessed her with eleven grandchildren. She attributes the strength and courage to leave her abusive first husband to God, and also knows He was there for her battle to survive colon cancer. Today she shares her truth that with God's grace, anything is possible.

Jerileigh Farrell

To Be Continued

I imagined each dusty step of the barefoot walk up the gravel road to the third and last road in this run-down trailer park. First passing four trailers to my right, I reached the fifth trailer—yellow with a red porch. I used to love that red porch.

    I went inside, through the dark and musty living room, and into the kitchen with bare cabinets. Moving on down the hall, the first right is the laundry room, smaller than a prison cell. There I found her, a little girl, four years old. Wearing a white dress with little yellow flowers on it and a yellow bow, her hair was messy but in a little ponytail with a yellow ribbon tied around it. She sat on the waist-high counter, padded with the mat used to hold the freshly folded clothes, across from the washer and dryer. I was back in my first bedroom.

    Now I'm almost fifty years old and in therapy, and my therapist suggested I visit my inner child. I had a tea party with the little girl in the laundry room, an experience she never had. I imagined I sat behind the little barefoot girl, put my arms around her, and hugged this memory of my young self. I saw myself giving her a hug like she'd never had before, as tears rolled down my face, then turning to her so I could see her face as she smiled.

I vowed, "One day you will smile again and mean it. One day you will hold your head up high and know that you did nothing wrong. You will know that what was done to you was not just wrong but wretched and hellish. You will break through and find peace and forgiveness, not only for those who harmed you but, most importantly, you will find forgiveness for yourself." I hugged her once more and then left her in that laundry room before walking back down the gravel road, still barefoot.

When I opened my eyes, I believed everything I had uttered in that sacred moment with my inner child in that laundry room.

Today I am safe. Today I am healing. Today I have peace. Today I am OK. How I endured so much trauma is by the grace of God, and *I embraced the suck!* This term means we have to feel the pain (the suck) in order to heal.

Just five years ago I suffered a heart infection called endocarditis, caused by the needles I used to shoot dope. Unresponsive, I was lying on a gurney in the emergency department inside a deep fog. As they worked on me, doctors and nurses moved in slow motion, as if in a ballet, passing the paddles for the defibrillator. I was in unimaginable pain and praying to a God that I didn't even know, begging Him, *Just take me now because my life is meaningless.*

Then, from behind the doctors, appeared Mike, my brother who passed away two years before. He moved slowly toward me as I stretched my arms toward him, begging him to take me with him. Mike smiled and said, "God's not ready for you yet. You have a survival guide to give away. Baby girl, I love you."

He turned and walked away, and I knew I needed to recover and change my life. But in the core of my wounded soul, I still didn't believe that I even had a heart. Yet, if Mike was hanging with God, there *must* be a God.

As a little girl, I was told God punished our family because I was bad, so my mental commitment to change my life didn't lead to instant success. Although I didn't stay clean and sober right then, I took that message from Mike with me—that I have a survival guide to give away. I was clueless what he meant, but it stayed with me. I knew I was going to have to fight and fight for my life.

Today I laugh when I see how hard God tried to get through to me. He sent so many "angels in skin" who helped me on this journey. But I was oblivious to the messages. It was like He needed to slap me in the head with a two-by-four so I would hear His words.

I was so stuck on doing it my way. My soul was dark from years of abuse, drugs, and alcohol. I no longer cared what I put in my body as long it meant I couldn't feel the dark terror in my soul. I hurt people. I didn't keep friends longer than I needed them. I was miserable and had pushed everyone away. I didn't know how to be a friend.

And yet amazing people have been put into my life who taught me that I am loved. My soul grows lighter as each day passes. In treatment, I met a pastor who prayed for me. That night I got on my knees and prayed for the first time. When I opened my eyes, kneeling next to me was another woman from this inpatient program. I was so overtaken by emotion, all I could do was hold her and cry. I heard God loud and clear that night, telling me, *"Courage is just fear with a prayer!* You must be courageous!"

The following year I stayed clean and sober, but it was a fight: just me, God, and Chaos, my pit bull who has gone to hell and back with me. We began that year homeless in February. The only place I could think of staying was at my late brother Mike's house. I knew I could knock on the door and my sister-in-law would take me in … but that was continuing my old behavior, addict behavior. They had a run-down barn with barely a roof, and I had warm clothes on and a comforter for Chaos, who lay on top of me, keeping us both warm. The snow was falling through the roof, and it was freezing but safer than anywhere else. I knew I had to go through this struggle so that I would never want to go back to the lifestyle of addiction.

Within a few days, I was accepted to Healing Action, an organization for survivors of commercial sexual exploitation. Accepted because at four years of age I had been kidnapped and trafficked, I received trauma therapy, case management, and a peer specialist. I had a psychiatric nurse practitioner and a peer specialist at Assisted Recovery Centers of America. These people were some of my newest "angels in skin." Each taught me how to embrace what felt ugly or challenging. These angels taught me how to embrace memories of terror and trauma and heal. The staff at Healing Action also helped me find my own home, which saved me from the homelessness I had faced for more than a year.

My lifestyle was limited by Neurological Functioning Disorder, which is a form of complex post-traumatic stress disorder (CPTSD). My body would paralyze in fear: alert on the inside, but I couldn't talk or move. I'd forget how to breathe and then pass out. Once I was unconscious, my body would take over and start breathing again. These episodes could last up to six hours, disabling me enough to carry a Life Alert fob and leaving me unable to drive.

Knowing clearly that I didn't want to go back to my old life, I fought. I taught myself how to stay busy and learned I'm an amazing artist. I create beautiful art with leftover construction materials, and I paint and sculpt.

Uncovering that talent brought me to God, giving a sense of love that a father would give, and I had longed for a father my whole life. Finally, I was comforted by my father. Through my angels, God led me to a life where I became comfortable in my own skin. Two more of those angels were friends, Becca and Liz, who walked beside me, and I with them through all our recovery journeys.

Oddly, I feared the day I would regain everything I lost to my addiction—material things, such as a house and furniture. Fear that I would repeat the cycle and lose them all again gradually gave way to the realization that, as long as I keep God in my heart and continue doing the next right thing, the cycle will end. When active in my addiction, I didn't actually *lose* those material things. I gave them away like I gave myself away. Piece by piece.

In the end, it was forty-six years before that little girl fully felt the gifts and blessings that God put into my life. I know that God sent Mike to me in that emergency room for a reason, telling me to give away my survival guide. Because He did, I learned to become of service to others. Today, I dip my hands into the darkness of addiction to help pull others out of that hell. God has asked me to find the best version of me, even if I don't know who she is *yet*!

Now I am of service to God, volunteering and being that "angel in skin" for others. And I live loudly because I spent so much time hidden and quiet. Learning who I am is such a beautiful revolution, and I evolve each day.

So, *to be continued …*

Jerileigh Farrell was born in Lexington, Kentucky. Her mama moved her and her brother to the St. Louis area when Jerileigh was four years old, but she has kept her Kentucky twang. She is now the proud mama of three adult sons: two in St. Louis with her, and the oldest in Arizona. Jerileigh loves that she has become an artist in many ways. She paints and sculpts but also loves the art of working with others in addiction. As she creates beauty, she also grows closer to God, learning to listen to His words. Jerileigh is working on a memoir that will soon be published. Her hopes and dreams are unlimited, including being a voice for the sexually exploited and survivors of sex trafficking. Still feeling she is at the beginning of her journey, Jerileigh already knows it's the journey that is important, not the destination.

April Keubler

From Surviving to Thriving

Growing up in the 1980s as a Gen X kid included a wide variety of experiences that shaped my life. We played outside all day, and our parents didn't know where we were. We drank from the water hose, splashed in puddles, made mud pies, played on metal playground equipment, and did whatever we could to keep ourselves occupied. When the streetlights flickered, our parents eagerly awaited our arrival home. Our rotary-dial phones were connected to the wall with a wind-up cord that would tangle if we moved too far. We shared phone time, and if someone was expecting a phone call, others' phone time was cut even shorter. To reach anyone outside our area codes, we paid per minute for long-distance phone calls. Away from home, we used enclosed metal boxes that required quarters to make calls (also known as phone booths). There was no social media to occupy us or hide behind. There was no texting and no internet, which meant that nothing about life moved rapidly. Even our planned after-school playground fights were a waiting game.

Gen Xers' futures were also molded by bullying. Bullying happened in person; kids were mean to your face. Teachers were not trained to respond to the emotional results of bullying. The powerful impacts on children's and teens' mental health were swept under the rug. The thinking back then was that the wounds of the psyche would vanish and needed no discussion.

Counseling was not as prevalent as it is now. We all thought that if someone was diagnosed with a condition, there was something *unquestionably* wrong with them. My childhood consisted of a different set of problems. Regrettably, *I* was the force of intimidation to be reckoned with. I had a chip on my shoulder and a Teflon shield nobody could penetrate.

One problem with being a bully is the loneliness that sits in the pit of your stomach like you swallowed your childhood baggage whole. Not allowing anybody to hurt me *physically*, I was also not going to allow them to get close enough to hurt me emotionally either. Protecting myself from pain, I wore a façade of The Perfect Life, acting happy, bubbly, and carefree.

The anguish I truly felt was my secret. And that protective mindset covered me like the bed quilt that kept the night terrors at bay.

Yet I daily encountered feelings of despair and overwhelm at school and at home. I felt emotionally incomplete without a strong support system to help with those tornadic emotions. Full of depression, I was either angry to the point of confrontation or filled with teardrops I later shed in secret on my pillow. I wanted to *appear* strong because I felt my internal weakness overflowing. It wasn't until years later that I learned the expression "Hurt people hurt people."

Barely out of my teens, I married young and welcomed my first child within the first year of marriage. I was still learning who I was, but children changed my character and my responsibilities. I welcomed three more over the next few years and molded my life and mindset to fit the role of motherhood. I tended to my family, chauffeured everyone to all their sporting and school functions, coordinated Girl Scout meetings, freshened laundry, cleaned house, and played doctor, all while neglecting myself.

The sadness from my younger years continued, and my life became focused on surviving. Repeating the same routine activities daily brought little joy. Honestly, nothing in my life brought joy because I still had not worked through my childhood struggles. I played the role of martyr to my life and felt I must be an actor in the movie *Groundhog Day*.

Extremely unhappy with the constant cycling up and down of emotions, I also regretted the effects of my instability on everyone around me. I despised my dysfunctional patterns yet was clueless about how to change them. *What is the point of just existing?* I thought. Looking through eyes glazed by sadness, I could not see the many blessings around me.

Over these difficult years, I also searched for self-acceptance and a life purpose. The self-improvement journey led me to church groups and involvement with community groups and nonprofits. Self-acceptance also meant that I educated myself with a bachelor's degree. These external activities kept me busy but did not address the underlying issue of past trauma and emotional turmoil.

Trapped for years in my own mind games, I finally sought counseling and learned about forgiveness. I learned that forgiveness does not release the people who hurt me from responsibility for their actions, but it releases me from my entrapment in obsessing over the wounds. I also learned the necessity of self-forgiveness. I forgave myself for the moodiness, for wronging others, for not being the perfect parent, for continuing the generational cycle, and for not accepting life as a gift.

My healing continued with expanded self-awareness. Soon, I realized that the journey of self-discovery and growth continues every day, in small moments, not only through catastrophic events. These brief lessons teach and guide me into the attainable steps that shape my future. I've learned I always have a choice to wallow in pity or look for learning opportunities.

Certainly, counseling didn't "cure" me of all my insecurities and emotional wounds, but it led me closer to becoming the best version of myself.

I soon found more healing and happiness as I continued the search for my life purpose. During this time, I explored different job opportunities, and those experiences led me to my passion and a career that uses my talents and allows me to serve as a guiding light to others. Today, I find joy in seeing dreams of home ownership come true for those whose hopes were fading into "that'll never happen." I bring deep knowledge and extensive experience to guide and counsel homebuyers and sellers through what can be a surprisingly emotional process.

Carrying my heart on my sleeve meant that when my energy was low, others felt it; my emotions changed the mood in a group. And when my energy was high, I could exhilarate an entire room. I can't fake that upbeat energy, though I tried for numerous years.

My career path invited crazy-long hours and burnout. As I still hadn't delved into my past to reach the root cause of those violent emotions from my youth, I overworked myself instead, networking constantly, and never pausing for the support I needed. Avoidance and *busy*ness were continued "solutions" to avoid my internal problems.

I didn't meditate or ruminate on the past but found myself again on a repeating loop, just existing. I had high goals and expectations for a successful future, and I intended to do everything I could to reach them. That meant never being home and being emotionally unavailable. But working and staying busy to stay numb is not productive; that lesson has taken me years to learn. Constantly running toward external goals wore me out and brought me no closer to joyfulness.

Through networking and building close friendships, I've become increasingly aware of what it means to be authentic. Finally, I clearly see that my familiar habit of ignoring problems no longer serves my growth mindset. Ready to face my closet full of skeletons, I committed to a certified training program of the unconscious mind. This program, neuro-linguistic programming (NLP), helped me relearn that I am human, with all the same stumbling blocks and moments of genius most of us find, and that my past does not define me. Suddenly, I saw the world through the lens of grace. Anger that once defined me no longer characterized my life. Little irritations no longer triggered emotional outbursts, and my relationships began to improve, at home and everywhere else in my life.

I've learned that my wellbeing *is not* an afterthought; putting myself first *is* a priority. I now realize the need to listen to my body; it tells me when to rest and when to be active. I've learned that it's OK not to attend every function, to say no to some invitations. I allow myself downtime and appreciate the blessings around me. I begin my days with gratitude and affirmations, and I show up every day with the best version of me.

So here I am, telling some of my story, a story that was trapped deep inside for far too long. I know that God has a way of bringing us through trials so we can help others. Talking about once-hidden and shame-filled emotions freed me from the bondage of my past. I am human. Emotions may still get the best of me when I least expect it. The difference now is that I don't pretend the feelings away. I know to reach out to others when I'm plagued by negative thoughts. Talking about my story fosters deeper relationships and encourages others to open up as well.

Now I see that life is too short to give my time to everyone and anyone. Today I am more intentional in my choices of who *gets* to share my time. Those closest to me have walked with me through these years of healing and growth. And with anyone new, I refuse to pretend I am someone else or to play a role to please them.

With hindsight, I can see that everything in life is a choice. I can *choose* to play the martyr, pretend to be someone I'm not, or grow from experiences. I can live for healing awareness of how past traumas created my character. A friend once said that choice is power and suffering is optional. I can always blame others or take the necessary steps to define how I will shape my future. Content now with my past, present, and future, I don't need all the answers. I don't need perfection, and I certainly don't need to hide behind the sadness I once felt.

I've found my way back to my family while balancing my career with the rest of my life. Finally addressing my past molded me into my truest version. My hope is that my example will help others commit to self-care and to share their struggles. I know I don't need to hide in the shadows of what I once believed. I know my story carries an impact for those around me; my experiences are meant to be shared. Every day, I simply ask myself, What are the next necessary steps to continue healing?

April Keubler is a seasoned real estate entrepreneur who thrives on the dynamic intersection of family life, professional excellence, and personal growth. With a passion for helping others achieve their real estate goals and a commitment to ongoing learning and development, she has garnered numerous awards and accolades for exceptional performance and dedication to client satisfaction in the real estate sector. From achieving top sales rankings to receiving recognition for outstanding service and results, April has earned the trust and respect of both her peers and clients. With a focus on innovation, integrity, and excellence, she is committed to helping individuals and families achieve their dreams of homeownership while supporting their continued growth and success. April constantly seeks opportunities to expand her knowledge and skills through coursework and certifications dedicated to personal and professional growth.

Marcia Rodriguez

Knock, Knock. Who's There?

That summer day started like most. I woke up, took my daughter to summer camp, started cleaning the house, and did some laundry. But this day turned out to be no ordinary day. In fact, it proved to be one of the most traumatic days of my life. I suffered unimaginable betrayal and began to question everything and everyone around me. Anxiety and depression soon crept in, and my soul darkened. Fear dominated my every day. I went to bed every night and woke up every morning panic stricken. Challenged on many levels, this was a "dig deep for strength" passage in my life, and it changed me forever.

I heard a knock at the door and opened it with no hesitation. Why wouldn't I? In the open doorway stood a short, kind-faced, dark-haired man. He introduced himself as Charlie Round, said he was with the FBI, and asked for my husband. Initially, I thought, "This guy must be mistaken." But why would he know my husband's name?

I realized something serious was happening, and immediately my body began to react. I felt a cold chill run up my spine, my heart started racing, and my knees started to buckle. My stress response kicked in and, never mind the fight or freeze modes, I wanted to run far and fast. After that, I only heard bits and pieces. It was like when adults spoke to Charlie

Brown and all he heard was "Waa Waa Waa." I'm pretty sure I was having an out-of-body experience.

Then the phone rang and brought my body and soul back together. It was my husband, Donald, saying he was on his way home. Something in the tone of his voice raised the hair on the back of my neck. Why was he coming home four hours earlier than usual? I told him about the visitor standing on the porch, and he said he would be home in five minutes. Special Agent Charlie Round, my new friend, continued to wait.

Finally, Donald arrived, and the hard truth began to unfold. Nothing could have prepared me for what I was about to hear.

Donald was Vice President of a small-town bank and well respected in the community. Most people knew him on a first-name basis. He was raised in a wonderful family that loved him and was involved in the local church; he was everything I had looked for in a husband. I thought I knew him, but as the day unfolded I realized that I didn't know him at all.

It had all started with Donald's relationship with one bank client. She was well connected, including politicians in Asia and Africa … and some of her other connections were shady characters: twenty-two, to be exact.

Then the affair began, and she gained influence over Donald. He wanted to make more money, and she was there to devise a plan and execute it. She wanted to entangle him, leave her husband, and God only knows what they were planning to do with me. I'm certain that I would have been tossed to the side too.

Until this fateful day, I didn't know the definition of an arbitrage, an investment strategy designed to produce a risk-free profit. Risk free? There's no such thing. There's always a price to pay. As they say, "If it's too good to be true, it usually is."

The sordid details were that Donald had committed $200,000 to such an investment. He didn't have those funds, so he created a fictitious loan and forged the signature of one of those twenty-two shady-character connections of his lover. To make sure that the shady guy didn't catch on, Donald made another loan in another shady character's name, to pay off the original loan. He did it over and over. The strategy was to move fast each time, ensuring transactions went through before the loans came due.

Then, during a bank audit, his fraudulent activity raised a red flag. He was on their radar; the bank auditors were watching him. Then the FBI caught on too. These twenty-two shady guys were involved in much bigger crimes, and their names were now linked to this small-town bank. Imagine that.

Donald faced twelve federal counts ranging from misappropriation of bank funds to moving money out of the country into a fictitious company bank account. This is serious stuff. With his mistress's connections to overseas banks, they had established a fictitious company. Then they started funneling money to an offshore bank account. It was a very complicated plan. Together, they could be rich. Life *was* going to be good … until the FBI showed up.

There were twenty-two characters involved in the arbitrage, but the picture was so much bigger. Some of them were involved in drug trafficking and other illegal enterprises, and the FBI was interested in building cases against them. They wanted Donald to turn over evidence, avoiding his own arrest at least for the time being. This choice would put my daughter and me in a very dangerous position, as these shady guys weren't above seeking us out and harming us. So we headed to San Francisco until they were all arrested.

I'd always wanted to go to California, but not like this.

By the time we went to trial, a year had passed. We had literally lost everything: we sold our home to pay for legal fees, and our marriage was irreparable. This high-profile case was headlined in many local newspapers, so we withstood constant shame and judgment. I felt betrayed, angry, and scared.

I had never felt so downtrodden, and I was surprised how many people approached me to talk about what happened. In my small town, people often weren't interested in how I was doing. They were more interested in getting the scoop and spreading it. I felt bad enough as it was, and most of the time their passed-on version was embellished. It was a lonely time.

Because Donald helped the FBI, his sentence was light. Mine was not; I had to live with the aftermath of his deceptions. I had to sink or swim. I remember sitting on the floor of my new apartment wondering how I was going to make it through this horrific time. I had both emotional and financial hurdles to jump. I was scared, but I had a daughter who depended on me. My decisions impacted her young life. My choices weren't only about my feelings; they would shape her life. She deserved better than the life that Donald's illegal actions had laid on her. She lost one of the most important relationships in her life. I realized that she, too, had been through so much, and in her I found the motivation for my turning point. I brushed myself off and moved forward. I knew that it was time to make life happen for us. And by standing alone, I began to find myself.

This time of my life was a passage of growth. I appreciated my new life and all the people who stood beside me. They meant the world to me, and I'm grateful for these lifelong, beautiful friendships.

I started a career in finance. It wasn't a profession that I would have chosen for myself, but it provided a good life for us. And life can be funny sometimes! I finished my career as a fraud auditor, part of a team that recovered money for lenders during the mortgage crisis. Isn't that ironic?

I often ask myself, Why? Why did this happen? Why was I so naïve? Why was I so foolish? These questions haunted me for a long time, but, looking back from my perspective today, I shouldn't have been that surprised. My childhood was turbulent: physically and emotionally abusive. I learned to not rock the boat because it came with consequences. So I swept things under the rug and accepted things as they were, trying to keep peace in a hostile environment.

When it came to marriage, I repeated that familiar pattern. So even though I had some suspicions about Donald, I was too intimidated to question anything. My inner child was scared.

Before, I felt like I was in a constant game of dodgeball, chucking and ducking my way through life. Now I realize this was a coping mechanism, allowing me to move forward and yet go nowhere. That version of life was exhausting. Through counseling, I learned ways to set boundaries without fear. It takes a lot of undoing and hard work. I am a work in progress but moving forward in the healing process.

Today, I help others who suffer from trauma. I work with a team of professionals who help people heal their trauma-damaged brains. It has been proven that trauma has a significant impact on our brains, not only psychologically but physiologically. The good news is that research reveals that the brain can be changed and the quality of life restored. When you change your brain, it changes your life.

I remarried twenty-six years ago. Although relationships are never perfect, they can be successful. He is an honest man, and I *appreciate* that. I don't question his trustworthiness because I don't have to. Marrying him, I also gained his wonderful, very large family, as he's the baby of nine siblings who are all very close. Family gatherings are boisterous and a lot of fun. I feel fortunate to be part of it all.

My daughter is forty-two now, but by age seven she had experienced more challenges than most of us experience in a lifetime. Although she lived all the chaos with me, it wasn't until much later that she fully comprehended the complexity of it all. She is a strong, honest, and caring person, and together we became survivors. She has blessed me with two awesome grandchildren.

That long-ago day, I had replied, "Who's there?" to the unknown knock-knock on my door. Now I know that it was not the FBI but trauma, recovery, and growth that stood on the other side. With thirty-five years of healing and building a new life now behind me, I clearly see that it was this new, stronger version of myself outside that door, knocking to be let in.

Oh … and I saved the best bit of my story for last. As Donald's trial came to an end, I learned that the last loan he forged was in his mistress's name. I have no doubt that karma exists.

Marcia Rodriguez studied Psychology at Southern Illinois University in Edwardsville, Illinois. She became interested in brain health due to a strong family history of anxiety, depression, and Alzheimer's. Marcia is a nationally licensed brain health educator and coach, licensed and certified through Amen University, and is certified in health and nutrition through the Dr. Sears Wellness Institute. She is also a National Academy of Sports Medicine–certified personal trainer. As owner and director of Neuro Strong, Marcia helps clients optimize their brain health. By changing the brain, which can heal regardless of age, traumatic events, or brain injuries, she helps people change their lives. Marcia is forever passionate about improving the lives of others.

Karyn Williams

The One That Got Away

I sat on my couch unable to move, obsessively analyzing this latest betrayal, trying to figure it out. I had given so much of myself while trying to make us happy—way too much, in hindsight—and here he was making a fool of me. I had never watched a Lifetime movie, and yet I was comparing my life to one. It was ironic, of course; but how else could I explain the turmoil I was experiencing? At thirty-one, I was a mom of two young children, pushed against my will onto an emotional rollercoaster with my soon-to-be ex-husband. This ride was completely in the dark with sharp, jolting turns and sudden drops. The shock factor was real, and dramatic was the best—and only—way to describe it.

Like many people, I never would have predicted my circumstances. While I wasn't the girl who pictured and planned every detail of her wedding growing up—my dress or ring were never top of mind—how I would *feel* being married was something I often thought about. I distinctly remember lying in my bed many nights, imagining how my future husband and I would interact. Laughter and happiness were part of every storybook scene. Quite simply, I wanted to love and be loved. What I envisioned is probably normal for many people, but based on what I witnessed in my childhood home, it seemed like a fairy tale. So, having dreamed a fairy tale *happily ever after*, I didn't want fighting, screaming, mental mind games, or severe emotional ups and downs. And yet that's exactly what I married.

In my defense, I did what I thought I "should." As the youngest of four, I usually followed in my older brothers' and sister's footsteps, lacking confidence in my own decisions and what *I* wanted because those were never encouraged or supported. I saw these people I looked up to getting married soon after college graduation, and to make sure I did the same, I decided it was OK to put up with emotional, mental, and verbal abuse.

I saw the red flags. They were huge, bright, and waving in my face constantly. I heard the deep concerns of my family and friends. But I wasn't able to get myself out. I feared being alone. I held on to the moments between us that made life seem good. Cancelling our wedding plans seemed unthinkable, and a decision I knew would leave me riddled with guilt. Worried about what people would say and how I would be judged, I gave up on the one thing I wanted most: a happy, healthy relationship.

His rage and explosive behavior were so intense and berating, I constantly felt hopeless and lost. My therapist, who I hoped would help me find ways to handle life with him, assessed him as a narcissist after they met individually. Even though I didn't really understand what being married to a narcissist meant at the time, I now realize the results included everything I experienced: manipulation, control, impulsiveness, emotional roller coasters that never settled, and verbal and mental abuse. And the key feature of narcissism is that the antagonist thinks they are doing nothing wrong and never admits to or apologizes for their actions.

I was pushing for necessary change he would never accept. I hold so many stories of nights spent crying and afraid, moments of confusion and betrayal, and a depression that I didn't even recognize at the time. Now, more than ten years after it all ended, I'd much rather share where I am today—yet that forces me to start when it was the darkest.

Our kids were four and one, and we had recently moved into our huge "forever home." My husband had just dragged me through a week of silence that began without warning when he finally broke the news that he wanted a divorce. He was not open to any kind of communication about what was happening, and I was enraged at how he handled it.

Every muscle in my body felt stretched beyond its limit to contain my intense emotions; my fury had no way of truly escaping. But I didn't fight. We had been down this road before, often during what should have been the happiest and most celebratory occasions. Isn't a honeymoon a safe bet for a truce? Not for us. Our near-constant and mutual threats to leave seemed real, but until now neither of us had acted on them. This time was different. Instead of trying to get him to stay or even talk, my mind and body finally surrendered so they could get a break from the constant stress. And yet truly unpredictable turmoil lay ahead.

I discounted my sister's theory that there might be someone else involved and attributed his quick decision to divorce to his well-known emotional blowups and impulsive behavior. I was wrong. There *was* someone else, and that proved to be the final blow.

I had already endured so much hate and fury from him, and yet he discovered this new way to hurt me: complete betrayal. I remember calling my brother that night I learned the truth, so hysterical that he feared leaving me by myself. My sister-in-law took the kids for me the next day, giving me permission to sit on that couch, immobile and obsessed, living my personal version of a Lifetime movie.

But why did I care when he was clearly not Prince Charming? Because this was *my* life, and, more importantly, the marriage I had chosen. I blamed myself for locking the kids in this traumatic isolation with me.

And the battle that followed his explosive departure streamed as that Lifetime movie in which I played a leading role. Feeling no remorse, his flagrant behavior escalated; the hate heightened. For months I woke up to lies and dishonesty, and was smacked in the face with his abandonment of our kids. His hateful words on my phone screen were the cherry on top of this toxic sundae.

And then his maliciousness began to fuel me, rather than drain me. At first I was driven by anger, and then, very slowly, anger evolved into the desire to rise above, to overcome, and to grow stronger. And I found an inner strength I hadn't known before. I leaned on a small support system, which was enough because I had myself too.

Music helped, and I can recite every song that became part of my soundtrack for this time in my life. Every time I hear them today, my heart fills with grief and strength at the same time. Music has always been a source of therapy for me, connected to both warm and traumatic memories throughout my life. This time was no different. Katy Perry's hit song "Roar" had just come out, and I took her lyrics on as my personal mantra. Every single word matched what I was feeling and going through, and it gave me the fight I needed.

I started making significant decisions on my own, like moving to an area where I'd always wanted to live, finding a job that made me happy, and choosing schools and nannies for the kids. With each decision, I grew stronger and clearer about what I wanted. I'd always labeled myself an indecisive person, but during this time I realized I simply never had the chance to *be* decisive; I always was controlled by someone.

The freedom of making my own choices felt powerful, and I embraced it. With each decision, from decorating our apartment to how the kids and I spent time together, I became increasingly confident. For the first time in my life, in my thirties, I formed my own thoughts and opinions about religion, political leanings, finances, and how to raise my children. I no longer parroted values I was told I should; I dug deep and asked myself how I truly felt about the world and my place in it.

I wish I could say I left this horrible situation on my own strength, but I was forced into this enlightenment. I hadn't grown enough to escape on my own, and that's OK. As long as I *accept* growth when it smacks me in the face, I can still reach a positive outcome. And I found peace in many ways: weekly wine nights with my two closest friends to laugh and cry and plan my future; taking time to relax, breathe, and imagine a new beginning; reading inspirational stories and quotes; releasing frustration and angst through workouts, runs, and listening to music. These tools protected me from being consumed by the dark clouds.

And I now live my original version of *happily ever after*. No, it's not dance parties all day and peonies that never die (yes, both are part of my version of perfect). But I'm now aware that even though that ideal doesn't exist, life still can be an amazing adventure. Investments in deep self-reflection and work to heal past trauma continue to this day. Now I am strong, self-assured, decisive, fiercely independent, and in a marriage that closely resembles my fairy tale dream.

In most lives, it seems, there is *the one that got away*. I'm tremendously happy that mine, when he left, opened the door to my true happiness.

Karyn Williams is a wife and mom of three children. More than fifteen years ago she left her short-lived journalism career for her dream of being a stay-at-home mom. And then she realized that wasn't actually *her* dream, but just what the women in her family had always done. When she started working again at a lifestyle magazine in St. Louis, it wasn't long before she became Editor in Chief, a goal since high school. Her other positions include lead copywriter at a digital marketing agency, director of communications and partnerships at an international nonprofit, and marketing director for a glass studio and arts district. Karyn also continues to make time for her first love of editing, through numerous freelance projects. Her life anthem continues to sing in her inner ear, repeating, "I got the eye of the tiger, a fighter, dancing through the fire 'cause I am a champion, and you're gonna hear me roar." ("Roar" © Concord Music Publishing LLC, Warner Chappell Music, Inc.)

Kerri Landis

The Worst Year of My Life

I stared up at the blackened, melted siding of my house and the cluster of burnt stuffed animals on the roof. "He lit the house on fire," I said redundantly. How many times had I asked our neighbors to keep their six-year-old off the rowhomes' common roof? But it could have been worse. With our house empty as we fixed it up to sell, the whole row could've burnt down. "This year really sucks," I thought. It was April 26, 2020. Little did I know how premature my statement was.

*****

I remember my last train ride from Philadelphia, fittingly on Friday the thirteenth of March. The journey was quicker than usual, thanks to all the platforms already shut down before the line closed. My boss decided I could work from home temporarily. The train's windows glowed in the evening darkness as commuters broke the strained silence with whispered worries. I spent the hour wondering how the institutions I depended on could shut down seemingly overnight.

When I got home, my husband and I decided we needed to make a move. "We've been wanting a place in the country," Joe said. "Do we want to be stuck *here* if they make everyone stay home?"

By mid-April, we had stored everything but the essentials in my in-laws' basement and moved into my husband's childhood bedroom. We were there when 2020 hit its explosively bad groove. My experience of the pandemic world seemed pretty different from my friends'.

April: "Don't be selfish! Stay home and stay safe!" one Facebook post screamed. We drove from my in-laws' to our rowhome, feeling like we were doing something wrong. "They'll understand we need to paint so we can list the house, right? Even though that isn't 'essential?'" Joe just grimaced.

May: "Another day at the office!" another post crowed, displaying a selfie of PJs and a lap cat. I wondered how much longer we could hang onto my husband's business now that he'd been locked out of his office at the retirement community for two months. Keeping the elderly physically functional wasn't an essential job, according to the governor. How could the government declare that any job wasn't essential to the person who depended on it as a livelihood? Added to this struggle was the news that our insurance company couldn't move our fire claim along. They couldn't send an adjustor—to our empty house—for fear of exposure.

June: "Being isolated is tough, but at least there's time for new hobbies! #SourdoughLife!" Cross-legged on the bed, I put my head in my hands. We had been stuck indoors with my moody in-laws for three months. They had closed their office to work from home and *never* left. My days became a smear of frustration as the bedroom, tiny office, and bathroom—all two steps away from each other—blurred together. Joe still wasn't allowed to work.

July: "I miss my kids, but this is for everyone's safety." The photo showed a mom and daughter, hands on opposite sides of a window. I bawled my eyes out for a few minutes as I took a break from packing our essentials yet again. After an argument, my in-laws decided we should move out. Where were we going to go? We couldn't afford rent with only one income. Joe put his hand on my shoulder. "Maybe we can stay at Evan's." I closed my eyes to take a deep breath and to wish for a friend who wasn't there.

*****

A highlight of my early adulthood was reconnecting with my childhood best friend. Rose and I grew up on the same block, having fun and getting in trouble all through school. We didn't stay in touch through college, but after graduation I looked her up and it was like we had never stopped. It wasn't long until Rose met Joe's childhood friend, Andy. Before we knew it, they were dating. The four of us developed an easy friendship, cooking weeknight dinners, hanging out on weekends. A decade passed, and by late 2019 Andy and Rose had grown apart. After a big argument, Andy moved out, and soon Rose didn't want to stay there anymore. The memories and emotions captured there were too overwhelming—so we helped fix up her house, and were by her side as she searched for a new home.

Soon, Rose started dating a new guy. She shared stories about his mysterious past that put me on edge, but she was enthralled. "Kyle is the anti-Andy! Just what I need."

With every contradictory story, my instincts were screaming that something was up with this dude. He was trying his best to be enticing, and it was working. One day, I met up with Rose. She was smoking a cigarette—a habit she had dropped more than fifteen years ago. "Does Kyle smoke?" I asked.

"Yep!" she replied. My heart sank.

"I'm a little worried about this," I said carefully, and not for the first time. "I'm getting some red flags. Are you sure this guy is good for you?"

Rose turned quickly to face me. "You keep saying this. I don't see it! Kyle is great and you're not being there for me. I don't see how we can be friends if this is how you feel." I felt sucker punched. She didn't see how her own behavior had changed, or how I was very *much* there for her by pointing out Kyle's shady actions. And that's how, right when I needed my best friend most, I found myself without her. Her new house was walking distance from my in-laws. It could have been an oasis during these past fraught, pressure-cooker months. But it wasn't.

After that sucker punch of a day, I began excavating my memories, looking back at our friendship. The more I scraped away the emotions, both negative and positive, the more I realized that maybe we hadn't been as good friends as I thought. I sifted through the past, noticing a recurring theme: I was the one who made plans happen. Rose was a willing participant, but the times she reached out first were few and far between. And who had restarted our friendship? Me. Maybe I had been pouring my efforts into a one-sided relationship.

*****

My eyes snapped open as music thumped next door. I watched August's morning sunlight filter through the blinds at our friend Evan's house. He had moved in with his girlfriend during the lockdowns and was letting us rent for a song. It was a refuge in the storm of 2020, and a breath of fresh air to have someone who actually cared about our situation extend a helping hand.

Meanwhile, my work was increasingly frustrating. It was evident that the husband-and-wife publishers weren't willing to hand over the editorial reins as promised, leaving me in limbo as half assistant, half editor. To gain some career satisfaction, I began moonlighting with John, an old employer who was starting a new publishing company. But at least I *had* a job. After six months of being closed, Joe's fifteen-year-old business was destroyed.

Now our main preoccupation was finding a house. It had been a month of driving hours away, hoping that *this* property would be it. As September wore away, the market shifted with the influx of people moving in-state. There were few houses in our price range, and they needed a lot of fixing up.

"We can't afford a place here," I said after a frustrating outing. "Maybe we should look in other states." Idly, I did a Zillow search in Florida and discovered exactly the sorts of houses we wanted in our price range. We had daydreamed about moving closer to a beach—somewhere rural, where we could make a little homestead, grow tomatoes, raise chickens, and finally get a dog. But it had always been just a daydream. After all the time and effort poured into building Joe's business, no way would we ever abandon it. Pennsylvania had taken that choice away from us, but maybe we could still make the best of a bad situation. I had accumulated some paid time off, so with Thanksgiving coming up, we decided to take a week to visit Florida and see if any houses hit the sweet spot.

Friday afternoon before my week off, my boss called. "I've got something to tell you," the older man said. "We aren't going to need you anymore, effective today."

My good mood vanished. Yet another person I depended on had abandoned me without warning. Suddenly, I felt the weight of each betrayal over the past year: my best friend; my in-laws; my boss; even the railroad and the Pennsylvania government. I thought about all the energy and devotion in various forms that I had poured into each relationship. But none of that loyalty had been enough.

Joe and I paced around the living room. "This is the last straw," I said. "I'm done with Pennsylvania and all these fair-weather friends. It's time to start over somewhere new. I don't know how … but we're going to Florida, and we're going to buy one of those houses."

I called John at my side gig, and he said I could start full time. Thank goodness we had reconnected! Joe and I drove down to Florida, went on a whirlwind tour of ten houses in one day, and put an offer on the first one we'd seen—a small home on ten acres of Florida Panhandle.

Four years later, Joe and I are finally in a good place. We work for ourselves, with no single boss who can leave us high and dry. I found out that Southern hospitality is real. We now have true friends who have taken us into their families—friends who are there for us and want to be in our lives. And we finally have those tomatoes, those chickens, and that dog.

Kerri Landis is a freelance nonfiction editor who specializes in helping authors polish their words into books and articles on a variety of topics, from how-to crafts and hobbies to personal memoirs. She earned her BA in English from Ursinus College in 2007 and lives in the Florida Panhandle with her husband, dog, and a whole bunch of chickens.

Jan Kraus

My Life As a Statistic

Each of us want to know we matter.

When treated as an intruder, the other, or not good enough, we feel lonely, invisible, frightened, and vulnerable. Everyone else seems to know a secret we don't deserve to hear. We retreat or, more dangerously, we defy those in power.

Affirmative action programs established in the 1970s were arguably a well-meaning partial remedy for discrimination, particularly in the workplace. Early in my career in computer technology, I learned employers could twist these programs to ensure those of us who are "other" did not benefit from affirmative action's essential purpose.

Ambitions

In school, I did well academically; however, my grades for behavior were dismal. Teachers rarely engaged my attention for long, and when they did I openly questioned what they offered. I carried on conversations with other students and could not sit still.

High school graduation was a joy. Excited to join the work world, my first full-time jobs as secretary and administrative assistant were fast-paced and action oriented.

A smart boss encouraged me to take up computer studies. I enrolled in night school, working toward an associate's degree. Work, school, and my social life satisfied and fully engaged my restless spirit.

My position as administrative assistant to the Director of Operations at "Small Bank" evolved beyond the usual job description to include computer programming. I was often asked to work odd hours, sometimes even in the middle of the night. I learned a lot and loved it.

"You should have been born a man," my boss said.

A compliment?

I was thrilled to accept a full-time computer programmer position at "Yee Old Railroad."

Statistical Deviant

"I am a very hard worker and you'll be happy with my productivity," I told my new boss in the interview. "I want to be challenged by my work."

"No problem with that," he said with a smile. "We'll keep you busy."

A big yellow school bus shuttled employees to and from the distant parking lot, and a bell rang at 8:00 a.m., dictating butts in seats. A little nervous, I didn't notice I was the only female programmer.

Days went by. No assignments. I visited the boss.

"Hi, I am ready to go to work," I said with a smile.

"Oh, yes," he replied with an answering smile. "I will have work on your desk tomorrow."

More days went by. No assignments. Conversation repeated.

My restless spirit took over. On the big yellow school bus, I made friends with folks from other departments. A few worked in the office next to mine.

I hung out with those friends. I phoned anyone who had time to talk to me. I socialized with my reluctant computer cohorts. I walked the halls. I rode the elevators.

Weeks went by. The boss called me down to a conference room.

"We can't have all this time spent away from your desk and on the phone. We can't have you visiting with gentlemen from the office next door," he said.

I stared at him, maybe with my mouth open.

"I told you when I interviewed: I work hard. I want work."

He repeated his cautions. I repeated my appeal.

"Come by this afternoon and I'll have something for you."

Days went by. Weeks went by. At my third time called to the conference room, I almost looked forward to being fired.

"Do you expect me to sit at my desk with a pencil in my hand and pretend to be working?" I asked.

"Yes." And he meant it.

"Well, you've got the wrong girl." I got up and left him sitting there.

The realization dawned slowly. I was an affirmative action hire. I was female, not valued for my potential, my work ethic, or my skills. I was lesser than, a government statistic.

The next day, a different boss, Barry, called me to a different conference room.

"I hear you are a troublemaker," he said.

Oh my, the truth!

"Wow," I said. "Maybe if I had some work to do, I wouldn't be such a problem."

"I'll get you work." He pointed at me. "But if you give me any trouble, you are gone."

"Thank you," I said.

Barry kept his word. From that day on, I was occupied and productive. Barry was happy. I was happy. I stayed for several years as I pursued my Bachelor of Arts degree at night.

Statistical Prisoner

I left Yee Old Railroad for a programmer position at a large corporation where a few other women were included in a larger team. Initially the work challenged me. I took on an interesting software system, solved its problems, and implemented solutions. I was asked to maintain that system. But only one focus, one application, could not satisfy my restless nature.

I found a position with more pay and greater responsibility with "Big Bank." My earlier job at Small Bank had been great, so I had high hopes.

"I am a very hard worker and you'll be happy with my productivity. I want to be challenged by my work."

"No problem with that," my new manager said with a big smile. "We'll keep you busy."

I quit my other job. But in my first hour at Big Bank, signing papers for Human Resources, their representative pushed the last sheet across the table, a contract. If I quit Big Bank within one year, I'd owe them several thousand dollars.

"What is this?" I dangled the paper by a corner.

"We don't hire anyone in the computer department without a signed contract," the HR rep proclaimed.

I had no job. My savings paid my tuition and school fees. I felt uneasy but signed. After all, this was going to be a great job. Wasn't it?

Days went by with no assignment. I visited my manager.

"Hi, I am ready to go to work," I said with a smile.

"Oh, yes, I will have work on your desk tomorrow," he answered with a grin.

Oh my ... déjà vu!

I spent my first two weeks talking with Pete, my cubical mate.

"How do you record your time?" I asked Pete when time sheets were due.

"I have a project number," he said. I entered eighty hours on my time sheet as education and research. After all, my manager knew I had been asking for work.

Next morning I was called into a conference room.

"We can't have all this time charged to these categories," my manager said with a stern and unhappy face.

"You haven't given me any work."

"We can't have all this time charged to these categories."

I was perplexed and frustrated. Silence filled the room.

"Well, get me a project number," I said.

He sat back in his chair and smiled. "Oh, OK, I'll do that."

Sigh ... here we go again.

Over the next couple of months, he threw small projects my way, but overall I spent my time talking with friends on the phone, wandering the halls, and generally making my manager unhappy because I would not sit at my desk with a pencil in my hand and pretend to be working.

I sought legal advice. Big Bank's contract was enforceable.

Once again, I was an affirmative action statistic. I was to be invisible. I was to be quiet and demure. I was to be subjugated by management.

My self-worth challenged, my ego bruised, I was afraid. As a single woman, I depended solely on my salary for the roof over my head and the food on my table.

Seeking advice from male friends, I heard that I was a complaining woman. I should "tough it out" for the year. My female friends suggested I settle down, get married, and give up my work.

I no longer asked friends for advice. At work I hid my vulnerability with petty defiance. I acted like I didn't care. But really I was adrift: frustrated, lonely, frightened, and depressed. I began to doubt myself.

Escape

One day, a memo appeared on the employee notice board. "Big Bank will participate in the Miss Downtown pageant. Entries open to all female employees."

No! My ambition was to succeed on intellect and skills, not on my looks. I respect women who choose the path of beauty queen, but I never thought of myself as one of them.

Then I realized the contest was an opportunity to meet influential Big Bank executives. After the contest, I might negotiate a transfer. Teller, bookkeeper, or any other position would be better than sitting around for a year with no dignity, no consideration, no esteem.

Only two Big Bank women entered the in-house contest. We were asked to write and present a speech to public relations.

Next day, I was Miss Big Bank. My manager came by my cubicle.

"You didn't."

"I did," I said with a big smile.

I think he was afraid.

Then fate stepped in out of the blue, as it always does. Another company offered me not only a step up to systems analyst but more money. They promised to pay off my Big Bank contract if necessary but suggested Big Bank would avoid a damaging news story, particularly one involving Miss Big Bank.

I had a long, candid talk with Big Bank's public relations director. He understood. I felt vindicated.

I hung up my crown before I'd even worn it, and my runner-up became Miss Big Bank. Win, Win, Win! Big Bank accidentally looked good for what is now called inclusion. The runner-up was Black.

I gave two weeks' notice, and the HR guy who had slipped that contract across the table called to say my last paycheck would be withheld against *what I owed them* for breaking the contract.

I started my new job the next day.

New Horizons

Eventually I moved from working for a paycheck into computer contracting and then consulting. I gained project-based work, lost some long-term security, and felt greater pressure to perform. But more varied and challenging subject matter suited my nature. The only contracts I signed were with my clients. The computer field grew up, and more women joined the field.

Diversity is the spice of life. Diverse environments hold power for the individual, for our country, and for our world. Our fight for inclusion and equity has come a long way but is far from over.

To paraphrase former Israeli president Shimon Peres, the choice at the heart of leadership is to pursue big dreams and suffer the consequences, or to narrow one's ambitions in an effort to get along.

Join me. Let's all choose big dreams.

Jan Kraus built a successful career in Information Technology for more than thirty years. Then, from 2012–2014, as Adjunct Professor at St. Louis Community College, and in partnership with Stanford University and the Bill & Melinda Gates Foundation, she authored several modules for the first Carnegie Mellon Healthcare Foundation course. In 2023, Jan's short story appeared in the #1 International Bestselling *Perfectly Imperfect* anthology, and she added Neuro-Linguistic Programming (NLP) Practitioner Certification to her life skills. Her song "Space Age" was featured in 2019's *It's Time to Write a Song* album, produced by Kevin Renick. Jan's sci-fi stories were featured at the Geisel Library's "Short Tales from the Mothership" events in 2020, 2021, and 2022. Her short stories appeared in the 2023 and 2024 St. Louis Writer's Guild anthologies. Her poem with painting and flash-fiction with drawing were featured in St. Louis County Library and St. Louis City Library publications, respectively.

Kim Skief

Give Yourself Grace

"Gracie."

"Yeah, Mama?"

"The doctor told us why you're not feeling well."

"What is it, Mama?"

"You have brain cancer."

Long silence ... "Will I die tonight?"

"No, Gracie, not tonight."

Heaving as I attempted to hold in my tsunami of emotions, I turned my head away from my eleven-year-old daughter, my baby girl, who I lay next to in a hospital bed. *She can't see me cry*, I thought. *I must be strong so she knows there's hope. Her doctor is wrong! Less than 1 percent?! Scr*w him! My God is bigger.*

Little did I know the struggle awaiting us.

A merciless monster grew in Grace's brainstem and dominated our lives with ruthless abandon for the next three months. Our first radical decision came with choosing home care and natural remedies. Life became a rollercoaster ride of hope and despair as each temporary reprieve preceded yet another devastating loss of function. Loss of walking, speaking, multiple resuscitations, and hour-long, rage-filled, focal emotional seizures became our household reality. I still remember her last words, six weeks postdiagnosis. Barely coherent, she willed herself to say "Happy's Father's Day," despite her great frustration.

Grace's suffering broke my heart. As time wore on, the hope turned to exhaustion and despair on every level. Each day began to feel like playing a game of Russian roulette. Will today be the day she dies, or will this remedy help? Meanwhile, we did our best creating priceless memories but felt there could never be enough. Moments after she passed, almost three months to the date of her diagnosis, an unexplainable but fleeting peace washed over me and left me with a profound knowing that *love is the point*. A torrent of painful emotions quickly took the place of that knowing.

At first, the guilt, regret, and shame felt insurmountable, like relentless tidal waves taking me down, over and over. *It does not matter how much I tried to heal or love her. I failed unforgivably.* These thoughts haunted me. I felt untethered, like I was drifting. Nothing made sense anymore; everything was open to questioning, especially my faith. I mean, come on—God let her suffer, and my family too. And this wasn't the first time I had lost a child. After three miscarriages, I nearly gave up, then Grace was born ... hence the name. *God surely had a reason*, I told myself. And I narrowed that reason down to one of four options: God is incapable, uncaring, unwilling, or gives conditional love. I couldn't accept any of these choices, and so my soul-searching began.

My exploration started with me and God having a chat not long after I attended a grief support meeting for parents. Another mom in the meeting asked the group if we thought her son was in hell. Her question spurred this thought for me: how could we, as mothers, love our kids more than God? If this feeling of separation felt like it was killing me, then do I love my child more than God loves all his children? I told God in no uncertain terms: I will no longer tolerate anything but the truth because I would rather believe in a difficult truth than a comfortable lie. No more contradictions or platitudes for me. I longed for peace, and nothing would stand in my way. Only my soul knew the healing journey I was about to embark on.

When I wasn't crying, screaming, or filled with anxiety, I became obsessed with reading, reflecting, and journaling. Ultimately, my decision to pursue peace meant walking away from my marriage, my home, my surviving children (who chose to stay with their dad), and eventually my Christian faith and many friends. I stepped bravely into an existence with no foreseeable future, unemployed and without a home. This began my two-year rollercoaster search for a peaceful and stable home and job.

I plodded along, still trying to get my bearings. After nearly two years of suffering and deep reflection, I came to terms with God as unconditionally loving with no strings attached. Yet I was still stuck on the idea that God loves me but doesn't like me. For a couple more years, I tried to sort out how to make sense of an unconditionally loving God who allowed my daughter to die a brutal death. I resigned myself to the thought, *I'll understand when I'm dead.*

Four years into grieving, my own stage 3 colon cancer stepped into the picture just before the pandemic started. The diagnosis hit me like a ton of bricks; my fear, anger, and confusion were intense. I wondered, *How did this happen? I'm such a healthy eater.* I refused, however, to accept the thought "life is unfair," as I had when Grace passed. No, that belief doesn't serve me. *But how do I go on like this?* Grieving my daughter, three job changes, four moves, a divorce, letting go of long-held Christian beliefs and much of my support system, empty-nest syndrome, world hysteria … and now cancer. I felt exhausted. But I thought, *If I can watch Grace struggle through brain cancer, I can do anything.*

The kindness of others freed me to invest my energy into healing myself, so I decided for the second time in four years to delve deeper into my spiritual journey. I knew I needed to have a better understanding of what I believed, and I allowed my curiosity to draw me toward certain spiritual books. My mind expanded in ways I had not even considered. I really dug into healing myself internally and decided to give zero f*cks for people-pleasing. I am grateful to say that after four years and counting, I am healthier than I have been in years.

My "near-death experience" caused me to embrace life more fully. So, at nearly fifty years old, fueled by my passion for holistic health, my intuition led me to become a wellness coach. Drop the mic. My spiritual depth and healing skyrocketed. I realized then that my victim mentality held me in a pattern of unhelpful thoughts. I was choosing a badge of honor "earned" with my trauma.

For years I "won" the game of Poor Me conversations people often have. Everyone immediately agreed my situation was the worst imaginable, topped only by war. I even told myself that my trauma was as bad or worse than war veterans because of what I'd witnessed. It took me years to unlearn that belief. I slowly came to terms with the idea that everyone is hurting and that pain is pain, trauma is trauma. How did it serve me to hold onto this story of "my life sucks more than yours"? My eyes were opened by one of my coaching tools. My victim story served me because I fed off the attention it gave me.

This realization kicked my guilt and shame into gear. Oh, so familiar ... I've steeped in guilt and shame most of my life, starting with my Catholic upbringing and followed by my Protestant faith with a new brand of guilt and shame. I beat myself up but also realized on a deeper level I was seeking a kind of love I felt incapable of giving myself and truly unworthy of. I still thought, *I can't unconditionally love myself because ... well, I'm not good enough.* I had not yet fully embraced who I am as a conscious creator of my life, but my eye-opening experience laid the groundwork for major reconstruction.

My next moment of reclaiming my power came two years postdiagnosis. After a movie date, my adult son shared he felt I abused him as a child and then announced an indefinite need for no contact. Wow, I felt as if I'd been run over by a freight train: sad, anxious, depressed, ashamed, and angry all within the first twenty-four hours. Then one of the spiritual books I had started reading but never finished called my name, and it brought the next layer of healing.

I began to accept all of me and took full responsibility for my life. My big breakthrough moment came when I eventually awakened to the following truth: We are all unconditionally loving, creative, powerful beings longing to remember our true nature. Eight years after her death, I recognized Grace's passing was a gift. She entered this world (as I believe we all do) knowing the impact she would create, and feelings of gratitude and joy flooded me.

I can truly say I am grateful for all my experiences because I finally understand they are all "pointers" directing my path forward. All my challenges revealed to me that I am not, never was, nor will I ever be separated from unconditional love. The stories or limiting beliefs I created based on my conditioning were the only barrier in my way of knowing love never fails. Even the religious trauma I experienced during my days as a Christian served a purpose, as it shone a light on my soul and allowed me to see my true nature. Now I know: We all are an extension of a loving, powerful creator. We are each responsible for ourselves and for the lives we choose to build. We are the thoughts we embrace, which feed the emotions we experience, from shame to joy.

I see trauma as an opportunity for self-compassion and growth. I am inspired to encourage others to learn to love themselves unconditionally, as I am. I have come to believe that, although people may need guidance or assistance to learn to love themselves, no one needs to be saved because we are all capable creators. Each of us has the opportunity and responsibility to reflect within and determine which thoughts create love instead of suffering.

Kim Skief is a successful holistic health and spiritual empowerment coach certified by the National Board of Health and Wellness Coaching. Kim helps women grow their inner peace through self-compassion. She nurtures mindful self-care practices to create a life filled with joy and good health, with a specialty in gut and hormone health. As a recovering people-pleaser who has healed layers of fear and shame within herself and others, she shares hard-won wisdom about radically loving oneself. Her journey of self-love started with embracing holistic nutrition, then alternative medicine, releasing repressed emotions, and eventually metaphysical healing. She healed her stage 3 cancer and Hashimoto's thyroiditis. Kim believes we're all whole, creative, and unconditionally loving powerful beings. From the Midwest, and well-traveled over half the United States, Kim is drawn by natural wonders and sees nature as her "church." She enjoys hiking, camping, writing, reading, dancing, and inspiring others through teaching.

Stella Webb

Holy and Healing

As a child, I never knew which mother I would wake up to. Would she be sitting quietly at the kitchen table drinking coffee and reading a newspaper? Or would she be raging at the world with me as the designated punching bag? And I was always the punching bag. There were so many days of my childhood when she was having one of her anger-fueled fits, when I would wake up to her screaming at me and then go to sleep with her still screaming at me that night.

The words she said to me … oh my, those words. Vile words I wouldn't even whisper in the ear of an enemy she screamed in my face, my own mother a monster more frightening than any devil from the pits of hell. Her face, red and twisted with anger and malice, is the recurring nightmare that for years woke me in the night covered in sweat and tears.

Sometimes during these verbal assaults my little body would start shaking uncontrollably. As a little girl, I didn't know what was happening, but as an adult I now understand that my nervous system was overwhelmed by the trauma, leaving me in a state of mental collapse. After these severe episodes, I found it difficult to make sense of anything in my head. It was as if the connections in my brain that helped me function were severed, leaving me a walking zombie until it subsided again after a few days.

The physical violence was just as brutal. When I was three or four years old and my mother was angry at something other than me, she knocked my head into the knob of a door until my white-blonde hair turned red. I had marks on my arms almost every day from where she grabbed my arm, her fingernails sinking into my skin as she spewed vile words into my face. Belt lashes on my back and buttocks were so deep and oozing with blood that it took weeks for them to heal. I endured bloody lips and ringing ears from slaps so hard I couldn't think right for a few minutes. I lost my hair, pulled out in chunks, and carried so many bruises. I cannot remember a day during my childhood when I was not bruised.

Fear reigned in my little heart through my entire childhood. The last place a little girl wants to go after school is to the very place she fears more than anywhere else in the world. Yet I had to go there every single day, so I lived in perpetual survival mode. I learned to watch every single micro-movement she made, study every single passing expression on her face, just trying to stay safe.

I always assumed I would end up dead at the hands of my own mother. This is a type of fear that most adults will never have to know, but I lived with it every day as a child.

As a young adult I could recall the physical and verbal abuse without breaking down. But the emotional abuse continued to haunt my memories. One particular incident stands out to me more than others because of how deeply it hurt.

We were walking down the street one day—my mother, my brother, and I—and my mom and brother were holding hands and skipping. They were so happy, and I wanted to join them. I timidly ran up and grabbed my mother's other hand in hopes of joining in the fun. My mother stopped in her tracks, glanced down at my hand in hers, and, with a look of total disgust, flung it away and then continued to skip and sing-song with my brother, leaving me standing all alone.

For a little girl of only eight or nine years, this event was one of the most devastating experiences in my entire miserable life to that point. Her heartless rejection confirmed what I suspected in my heart for a long time: that I was despised by my own mother.

The results of this emotional abuse have permeated every single relationship of my life: with my husbands (I am divorced and remarried), children, extended family, and friends—all tainted by my mother's rage. Trusting anyone else to be a safe harbor in life is still difficult because my own mother was not safe. This unwanted child became a broken adult, and I wondered if I had any chance of living as a well-functioning person.

I always knew the abuse was immoral, even as a little girl. Friends who saw the marks on my body as we changed for gym class threatened to call the abuse hotline. I asked them not to do that because of the horror stories I'd heard about foster homes. Better the devil you know, right?

As is true for so many other abuse victims, no adult stepped in to stop my abuser. Not family members (yes, they knew), not neighbors who had to have heard the screaming, not even members of our church community.

The abuse affected every part of my life. When I was a teen, I decided I would *not* be my mother. I would not raise my children with such violence. I would not live my life chained to the brutal suffering of the defenseless child I had been. I would find peace in this lifetime. However, I had no idea just how damaged I was or how long it would take to heal from the constant trauma I experienced during my formative years.

My Spiritual Experience

Where does one start when needing to heal every single crevice of one's being? I started right where I was. I was in my late thirties before it dawned on me that I was self-sabotaging. Soon after that realization, it became absolutely clear that I needed to heal, and that was the day I began walking a more intentional path to create a life of peace and joy.

I messed up time and time again. I continued to self-sabotage when I was unhappy because I didn't know how to create and maintain healthy relationships. I hurt those I love, and I hurt myself, over and over. I truly didn't know what it looked like to love or be loved. Some days, I felt so broken and lost.

However, I was determined. So, little by little, tiny step by tiny step, I began to heal those inner wounds, and this is what eventually transformed my entire life.

I have always been a very spiritual person, feeling a deep connection to the Divine. This profound spirituality provided the necessary fortitude to survive this childhood of horrific abuse. My deep connection to the Divine also gave me the optimism to believe my life could be better, and the determination to heal from my first sixteen nightmare years.

I spent my twenties and thirties studying various spiritual paths and working as a minister, pastor, and missionary in three Central American countries and in the United States, all of which helped reshape how I walk this earth in this lifetime. Now, as I look back on the whole of my spiritual path, I see several key realizations that helped with my healing over the decades. These realizations include:

1. I am not a human having a spiritual experience here on Earth, but rather a spirit having a human experience.
2. As a spirit, I chose to incarnate in this lifetime to learn lessons and to gain wisdom.
3. I also chose those with whom I would incarnate, such as family (including my mother), friends, and partners.

4. We help each other with these lessons as we each walk our individual paths for this human experience, which means sometimes we *are* the lessons for those around us.

In short, I now see our bodies as vehicles that our spirits occupy in this world so we can exist and interface in time and space. Our human experience is important. It's the whole reason we are here. Before we incarnate, we decide what lessons we want to learn. All lessons are important, including the ones I learned from my abusive mother. My *job* is to learn my lessons and integrate the wisdom I've gained so I can reach my highest potential in this lifetime.

After intentionally working for decades to heal those deep inner wounds from my ugly childhood trauma, I am no longer that vulnerable little girl who cannot understand how my mother could be so cruel to me. I have learned to distinguish between a perceived monster and those who do monstrous things. I know issues surrounding abandonment and betrayal are life lessons I chose for this lifetime. I have cycled through these lessons many times in many ways, but with the wisdom I've gained from the past, I now clearly see them when they come around, and attempt to navigate those situations in healthy ways. I have learned how to nourish my soul well, and I do this every single day as my healing path continues.

I live a life of peace now. That long sought-after peace is not a mirage anymore; it is how I live my beautiful day-to-day life. I am living my life to its highest potential and loving it. It is with great joy that now, at fifty-five years of age, I get to spend my days helping others as they heal their inner wounds. I remind them that they are spirits having a human experience. I create sacred space for others to feel safe, and I get to offer opportunities for them to learn how to nourish their souls so they, too, can reach their highest potential in this lifetime.

Still Perfectly I'Mperfect

Stella Webb's life has been a magical quest, a relentless exploration of the spiritual realms. She's not just a mystic; she's a facilitator for spiritual healing and renewal—a true cosmic multitasker. At Soul Sanctuary, Stella's meditation center, she teaches spiritual classes, tends to Reiki clients, and guides meditation sessions. She co-facilitates women's circles and conducts rituals; gives out spiritual advice like confetti; performs weddings, handfastings, and house blessings; and throws down some serious spiritual wisdom in public appearances.

Stella's got a non-spiritual side too. As a columnist for newspapers in South America, she tackled political and social issues, and also championed the cause for victims of domestic violence. Stella jet-setted across the world, raising the frequency around her as she went. She is a loving mother, a doting grandmother, a spicy wife, and a satisfied business owner. She loves her beautiful life.

Laura LaMarca

I Am Sick of Being Sick

I sat there at the dreaded annual physical just before my fiftieth birthday, feeling I had been smacked upside the head with a board. In fact, I felt this way *every* day I lived with two autoimmune diseases. I was already on thirteen prescriptions, and my doctor was telling me he recommended I add another. Why? Because the ones I was already taking weren't controlling my pain!

I remember shaking my head and saying, "Absolutely *not*! I am sick of being sick, and all your pills keep making me sicker! I am done with this sh*t!" For the longest time, I could not wrap my head around the fact that my doctors continued to prescribe one medication after another. But I do now, and that understanding launched my journey to a prescription-free life and inspired another launch: my own business to help others do the same.

I suffered from lupus, fibromyalgia, spinal stenosis, degenerative disk disease, and post-traumatic stress disorder (PTSD). During that time of taking thirteen prescriptions, I was also a type 2 diabetic with high blood pressure, high cholesterol, and migraines that required monthly injections. I was still in pain every single day of my life, even with the multitude of muscle relaxers, pain medications, and antidepressants.

Smoking marijuana was the only way I was able to relieve my pain.

We lived in Illinois then, and medical was legal, so I asked my doctor for my medical marijuana card. I obviously qualified due to my health conditions. The process to obtain my card … Well, I will be honest: it just sucked! I had no idea what I was doing, and no one helped me through the process. Then, after I received my card, I found myself still hurting after spending a lot of money at the dispensary.

I knew I was missing something important. None of the salespeople seemed to understand my questions or, frankly, to really listen to me. I was very frustrated and wondered if this was what my life had become: constant pain, days when even the slightest brush of the bed sheet felt like razorblades on my skin. This time was different; I had a glimmer of understanding that cannabis could be my saving grace, and relief from a cabinet full of prescriptions.

I did some research and found what sounded like a perfect fit for me: a program to become a Certified Cannabis Coach! A what? I wondered, *Is this really a thing or are people going to laugh at me when I tell them what I am doing?* And my answer was that I honestly didn't care anymore what people thought. I was doing this for me and me only because I knew there was more to life than popping pills and always feeling I had just survived a collision with a Mack Truck.

The first thing I learned was that God designed our bodies with an endocannabinoid system and that cannabis was the key to a healthier way of living. I had just been doing it all wrong. I went to my doctor and told him I was ditching Big Pharma and asked for his help to remove the medications properly. Thankfully, my doctor was a key to my success in helping me achieve my goals. I ditched my pain meds first because they had never controlled my pain, anyway. Then, with his guidance, I slowly decreased my load of prescriptions, one by one.

Before my fifty-first birthday I was prescription free, and it was *liberating*! Can you guess the other happy outcomes of a prescription-free life? I was no longer a type 2 diabetic, no longer had high blood pressure or high cholesterol, and was happier than I had ever been. And did I mention I shed seventy-five pounds? The best result is that this year I'll celebrate my fifty-sixth birthday and five years prescription free, living my best life.

Helping others live prescription free led me to open my business, Wellness Palooza, and that has been an incredible journey. I could not be prouder of the privilege of building this business with my daughter as we strive to educate people about cannabis, why it works, and how it works, guiding their informed decision on whether cannabis is right for them. I was desperately searching for someone like me when I began this journey. Now I am that someone!

Our business journey has not been easy to this point, but I am determined to build Wellness Palooza into a haven of healing never before seen anywhere. The biggest compliment we receive from our clients is, "Wow, nobody is doing this; we learned so much!" We have met some amazing hemp farmers in this industry, and they taught us more about the benefits of cannabidiol (CBD)and cannabigerol (CBG), which led us to learn to make our own products. My daughter and I can honestly say that without our farmers we would not be where we are today. We are grateful and loyal to them.

Being in the cannabis industry is not easy and surely not for the weak at heart. To be a woman in this industry is rare, and we've been dismissed and disrespected more times than we ever thought possible. But all of that has only made us stronger. I've spent my whole life fighting to be heard when nobody listened. Doctors didn't listen when I told them how *my body* felt. People I loved looked down on me when I started this business. I think having my teeth kicked in as much as I have in my life has made me the strong and determined woman I am today. I'm proud of me and what I have overcome, and excited to see what God has in store for me next.

Learning how to navigate the cannabis industry as a woman-owned business changed me, and more powerfully than I realized. Because this business was no longer only about being disrespected in the industry; it was also about being disrespected by my doctors not listening to me. Then it dawned on me … *No*, this pattern goes back farther than I thought and has been widespread, affecting many relationships. I've survived trauma that I pray I never have to endure again. I've been raped, molested, cheated on, lied to, lied about, and bullied by people I never thought would hurt me.

I don't know why I didn't pull up my big-girl panties and take back control of my life before my fiftieth birthday, but that doesn't matter anymore. What matters is that I did it and I've never looked back. I'm no longer that girl or woman who allowed people to treat me as *less than,* and it has been a long journey from there to here. However, this was a journey I needed to take.

Faith is the other big ingredient in my successful journey of surviving, recovering, and thriving. I joined an amazing Bible study group and started really developing my relationship with God, asking Him for guidance to heal from the trauma that had been making me sick. I no longer allowed others any control over my life, or any power to make me feel bad about myself. I decided to turn the reins over to God. Every day God takes me on a new journey, leading me to new clients and others who need our help, and it has been the most amazing experience in my life.

Wellness Palooza is my absolute pride and joy! We *are* completely different from any other CBD company, and I believe that is because of my journey … and my strong desire to help others feel the way I feel today. So many times, God sends us people we probably never would have crossed paths with. We don't question the where or why; we just welcome everyone with open arms. We are also blessed that some of the farmers we work with support our mission to serve those who cannot afford the typical costs of a cannabis regimen. They gift us flower at no charge, allowing us to offer products to those desperately seeking our help but unable to afford the cost. Been there, done that! And there's no shame here; we help anyone who needs our help regardless of ability to pay.

Six years ago, as I listened to my doctor telling me I needed a fourteenth prescription in my pill tray, if you had told me I would soon own a business in the cannabis industry, make my own products in a commercial kitchen in my basement, and help hundreds of people and their pets … well, I'd have thought you were crazy. H*ll! Some days I think I'm crazy for taking on as much as I do! But we just keep growing month after month, with people reaching out to us from all over the United States. Our CBD-infused dog treats, Coopie Snacks, are becoming a household name, and one day I will have our products in every state. But for today I am just grateful that I was sick of being sick, took back control of my life, and am now blessed with better health than I have ever enjoyed.

Laura LaMarca is a Certified Cannabis Coach and owns Wellness Palooza with her daughter Bailey. They are dedicated to helping others break through the confusion and frustration of cannabis in today's world. Laura and Bailey spend a great deal of time and energy developing their own products and are always researching new ways to help clients achieve a healthier life. They make all of their products and create individualized treatment plans for customers. In addition to helping humans, Laura has developed a line of CBD products for animals, striving every day to make the world a better place for humans and their pets. Wellness Palooza hopes to be a household name very soon, and, until then, Bailey and Laura are focused on breaking the stigma of cannabis. They want everyone to know—*We're Here to Get You Healthy, Not Get You High!*

Loryl Breitenbach

Going Out on a Limb Is the Path

"I'm going to go out on a limb here ..." Seeking advice from fellow health coaches, I pondered as I crafted how to pose my question. *Out on a Limb*—wait, didn't Shirley MacLaine write a book with that title? She was one of my first childhood idols. As a young kid, I loved to dance. I lived and breathed it. That and collecting rocks. (Sorry, Grandpa! Yes, I still owe you for the potholes I left in your driveway.) As a kid, loving dance meant I had to like pink. Every gift was pink, my dancewear was pink, and all the girls' dance bags were pink. No offense intended to you pink-loving readers; I might have thought it a great color if it hadn't been forced upon me. I was unsure if a girl who didn't like pink could fit into the dance world. One day, I saw Shirley MacLaine dancing on television. Kaboom! My mind was blown! She was not wearing pink, did not wear a tutu, and oozed talent, class, and sass, all while having the time of her life!

For the first time, I saw a dancer outside the stereotypical pink ballerina box. This new image of the strong, fun dancer sparked my realization that there was more than one way to be a dancer. I didn't have to fit in that limiting pink box called "dancer." I suddenly saw that I could *go out on a limb* to find my own style, my own favorite way to be me. I could express myself through dance with style and pizazz and inspire others like Shirley MacLaine had!

From that moment forward, I knew I could confidently continue following my love for dance. I danced my way through college, completing my Bachelor of Fine Arts degree, or BFA. Most dancers dream of moving to Chicago or New York, but that lifestyle never appealed to me. Perhaps I never moved to a big city because I never liked crowds ... Perhaps something else was waiting. After I married, I continued to perform and teach dance with other professionals in the town I grew up in: St. Louis, Missouri. But soon I went out on a limb on what seemed like a whole new tree. Along with dance, I studied anthropology in college and decided on a whim to take a summer course in archaeology (remember those rocks I liked as a child?). The following fall I took a paid position in archaeology ... You mean someone will pay me to look at rocks? Sign me up! I pretty much learned on the job. I transferred my skill for quickly learning choreography to learning processes, and my skill of noticing small details in choreography to noticing small details in artifacts. For a couple of years, I continued dancing, sometimes on stage, sometimes on breaks from dig sites in the fields of Southern Illinois.

I enjoyed wonderful opportunities during my time in archaeology, managing a team of students, cleaning and labeling artifacts, helping to collect data, and writing papers on collections. I was surrounded by people who had spent years studying archaeology, and I had the pleasure and privilege of reassembling giant puzzles made of tiny rock fragments from thousands of years ago! Stepping out onto this limb may have seemed like a random misdirection at the time. But looking back, I see that it helped me gain self-confidence. You see, growing up in the world of dance, I'd received many messages that dancers weren't as smart as everyone else.

This archaeology branch I climbed out on helped me see I had as much intelligence as anyone else, and patience too! Who else but me would enjoy counting, weighing, identifying, labeling, and researching hundreds of pounds of rocks, creating and completing a thirty-page Excel document like a kid counting their candy at Halloween? Of course, I've learned through the years that dancers are some of the smartest creatures on two feet, and I am privileged to teach dance to some of the smartest kids I know!

The most wonderful limb I ventured out on was starting a family. For someone who was so immersed in the world of dance, there was a mental block to get over before climbing out onto this particular limb. I feared I would no longer be dancing as much or might never return to my first love.

I can now scratch that worry off my list of concerns because here I am, twelve years later, still teaching dance. When my kids were younger, I wanted to ensure I could earn an income by working during their school day so I could spend time with them at night. The year came when they were both finally in school … then all heck broke loose when the pandemic hit. As soon as they started to go back to school, I enrolled in a program to become a health coach. Have you ever followed a nudge out onto a strange limb? You know, the kind of nudge that comes out of nowhere, doesn't make any sense, and though your friends are kindly supportive, they look at you strangely? That was this limb. It seemed different to some, but I somehow felt drawn to it. I'm not quite sure what I wanted to do exactly, but I knew I'd figure it out along the way.

Meanwhile, I would gain tremendous knowledge that could help my family and myself, and I hoped to share that knowledge with others. I worked hard all year, devoted time and energy, and even studied while on vacation. Graduation time came, and as I snuggled up in my robe and slippers to watch the online ceremony (on Zoom, of course), I should have felt happy and proud of myself, right? I was proud of myself for all I had set out to do, but there was this nagging feeling. What would I do with this newfound knowledge, and was it enough? Enough for what was coming around the corner …

Halfway through my education path, my youngest son became sick. After six months, we finally learned a diagnosis the same week I graduated. It is a type of immune disease seen in only five in 100,000 in the United States, and the numbers are climbing. I had learned all about autoimmune diseases in my training, but this one was not on the list. I wasn't sure what that meant for him or us as a family, but I knew we could take it one step at a time. It wasn't long before I saw why the universe had nudged me onto the health coach limb. That branch of my path prepared me for this next journey.

I became this child's advocate in the medical world. I learned how to keep food logs and identify food triggers. I meal planned and helped him navigate year-long food eliminations. We practiced mindfulness and breathing techniques as I sat beside him through countless blood draws, infusions, and endoscopies. Together we learned healthy ways to manage stress and anxiety and persevered as we found answers we weren't getting from the medical doctors.

Most importantly, we learned together how to show ourselves grace when the world seemed too tough to stay brave 100 percent of the time. Some days the answers were unclear to us or the doctors, and it felt like a storm of worry shaking our tree so hard I couldn't see which direction to go or what limb to reach for next. That's when we learned it was OK to take a break, be patient, let the winds of worry die down, and trust that the next best branch will appear.

I may not have taken the path other health coaches took, and that's OK. If I had not gone out on that limb, I would not have been prepared for what our family branch had in store for us. I have learned so much more through this health journey with him. All I have learned through this experience, combined with my education, has prepared me to help so many more on their paths to wellness.

Not knowing what to do with my health coaching education felt like I didn't fit in, just as I hadn't fit the pink tutu model of dance in my childhood. Thanks again, Shirley MacLaine, for showing me that one does not need to fit a single mold to make a difference. Shirley taught me it's OK to go out on a limb if for no reason other than I am called there. And it's OK if some limbs seem to lead only to joy and curiosity. It's OK not to know where I am headed. Sometimes that answer has been figured out for me. Now, I go where I am led, knowing the puzzle pieces will all fit together.

My son's health story is not over. There is no one-size-fits-all treatment plan for any individual. Not all dancers wear pink. Not all rocks are useless. Doctors don't always have all the answers. Not all immune diseases want to be cured the same way. When answers aren't readily available, I put on my climbing gear and explore new limbs whenever called. Everyone's journey to wellness looks different. Just as everyone's journey to find their calling or purpose looks different. If I don't go out on a limb occasionally and follow those nudges calling me to explore, I'll miss these chances to discover what life has in store for me. I keep on going out on that limb, finding the fruit that has been waiting for me!

Loryl Breitenbach graduated with a Bachelor of Fine Arts from Webster University in 2001, held many roles in the world of dance, and continues to teach in the St. Louis, Missouri, area. After adding certification as an Integrative Nutrition Health Coach through the Institute for Integrative Nutrition (IIN) in 2022, she is now an advocate for health, wellness, and functional nutrition. Applying integrative nutrition principles as she cared for her son's rare diagnosis brought direct experience in cooking for those with medical dietary needs. Loryl is currently training and honing her neuro-linguistic programming (NLP) skills. As a mom, she treasures her time with two busy boys, relaxing by the fire pit or the lakeside, or on movie nights, sharing the couch with the family pup. Loryl would like to thank her husband and older son for their patience and support in tasting all her new recipes.

Eliza Poe

Desperately Seeking Myself

As I sit staring out the window, the last several years spin through my head at dizzying speed: all the wishes to escape my weary reality and run away; all the wishes to be Madonna's character in the 1980s movie *Desperately Seeking Susan*, featuring a bored housewife who fantasizes about becoming a fun and carefree *Someone* she reads about in the classified section. What I wouldn't have given to be someone and somewhere else through all the turmoil. But there was no escape from my reality and no hope of rescue. I was buried in an avalanche of circumstances.

In May 2020 I received the worst news a parent can hear: "It's cancer." My sweet, loving son Christian, already living with special needs, was diagnosed with an incredibly rare cancer. For many years, just getting through each day had been a challenge, and now I was faced with this diagnosis and all that came with it . . . something my son wouldn't be able to understand because of his cognitive ability.

How was I to help him, I wondered, when I couldn't explain what would happen to him, what he would endure? I felt I could not let my son see my fear or sadness! He was perceptive and would pick up on it, and the last thing I wanted was for him to be scared. As fear devoured me, I swallow the flood of emotions and put on a brave face.

The four months between Christian's diagnosis and his passing were surreal. Our entire family experienced an amazing level of divine intervention, and I'm thankful for the Loving Hand that allowed my son to maintain both his activity and charming, jovial personality with minimal discomfort until the very end. Losing a child is unbearable, yet I feel blessed we were at home, as I held him in the comfort and safety of my arms, cradling his frail body as he took his last breaths.

All of his life, we had snuggle time every night before bed, and that night was no different. I wanted to take all his pain and fears, and for him to know he was protected. He gripped my finger with his hand, acknowledging my efforts, and I watched his bright eyes go dull as his spirit left his body. Having brought him into the world, I feel privileged to have been his escort home.

The aftermath changed our family forever. In fact, I spiraled into a year-long collapse of which I have no recollection. The crushing events of the medical journey, his death, the funeral, and family grief consumed me. Throughout Christian's life, I had felt I was defending against my ex's relentless attacks—in both daily interactions and far too many courtrooms—which nearly destroyed me physically and mentally. Waging a continual psychological battle takes its toll, and the effects get buried and leave deep imprints.

The end of my job as mom to my fourteen-year-old child with special needs was the end of an identity. I lost my five-year plan to bring my son into adulthood and instead became an empty nester in a blink. My existence, as I knew it, vanished.

The long-lasting relationship with my current significant other also dissolved as collateral damage. It's sadly common for couples to break apart under such strain. Though not his own child, he adored my son and coped with his intense feelings about his death by pretending it never happened. Yet I was the embodiment of the memory that now couldn't be discussed, so my grief became a target for him, burying yet another layer of pain and trauma into my body and mind.

As the one-year anniversary of losing my son arrived, I attempted to start pulling out of this devastation. I was seeking to purge my soul from the intense pain. My career, child, relationship, and stability were stripped away, and I needed to again find my purpose, to remember what is truly important in my life.

I desperately needed to rid myself of grief, but it enveloped me. Not a moment passed that my thoughts didn't swirl into despair. Sometimes I couldn't even breathe without reminding myself to. The loneliness overwhelmed me, though my wonderful family and friends helped in many ways, even as they grieved with me. I felt I couldn't lean on them; they needed their strength to mourn too.

Searching for inspiration to climb back into existence, I stumbled upon a quote from Bishop T.D. Jakes: "Somebody is in the hospital begging God for the opportunity you have right now. Step into your moment." And those words reversed my downward spiral. Here I am struggling to make it through a day, not knowing how to process my pain, and there *are* those who would take my place in an instant. That realization spotlighted my circumstances with a new perspective. When the gift of opportunity is offered, do you accept?

Yes. Challenge accepted! I have to find a way. I can't exist in this emotional vacuum anymore. But how do I move forward?

Three years after losing my son, a momentous event occurred in my healing journey, as the universe found another way to push me along. Since my son's passing, I've become quite the bird watcher, especially enjoying the cardinals for the spirit they embody. I'm particularly fond of the "teenager" cardinals with their mottled red-and-brown coloring.

As I sat working in my office, I glanced out at my deck and noticed a teenage cardinal had died after hitting the window. In the middle of a project, I didn't think much about it right then, but knew I needed to bury him by nightfall before the nocturnal animals found him. I wrapped up work at about dusk, grabbed a shovel in one hand, and carefully picked up the cardinal with the mottled colors in the other. He was a young one who lacked the experience of maneuvering around windows. I carried him down to the base of the tree and started digging.

When I was a youngster, we always buried our critters, whether a pet hamster, a bunny we found in the field, or expired birds under our windows. I can only imagine the array of bones to be found, cradled in empty tea boxes all over our yard. That childhood instinct carried me out to bury the unfortunate teenage cardinal. As I laid him gently in the hole and grabbed a handful of fresh dirt to cover him, the memory hit! I immediately flashed back to the moment I placed the urn of my son's ashes in the ground and spread the first handful of dirt. Overwhelmed and now sobbing uncontrollably, I finished covering the cardinal and ran into the house to collapse. I gripped the quilt made of Christian's t-shirts, wishing I could again hold him as tightly.

Why did I have such a visceral reaction during this routine bird burial? And then it occurred to me … I hadn't cried the day I buried my son. I imagined a bystander witnessing the event and thinking what a hideous mother I must have been.

The truth was, at that moment, I was numb. As though the burial wasn't actually happening. And I certainly couldn't let my dad see me break. Watching one of his grandsons being buried in the plot meant for him was more than my father could bear. I felt that if he witnessed the depth of my grief and the internal collapse I hid from him, he would have been irretrievably broken. I believed I had to be a pillar of strength for him. For everyone.

And yet I had no idea what pretending to be strong would cost me. My buried grief silently tormented me for three years until the toxic brew of sorrow spilled forth as I buried that cardinal. That episode freed me, releasing all the stored emotion I had hidden on the day of Christian's burial.

The pain and emptiness never fully faded, and part of me will be forever missing, with no way to fill that void. Acknowledging this fact and embracing the emotions that arise at random moments allow the healing purge to continue.

One of the most difficult feelings to overcome was the guilt when I started to find happiness in simple things again. Feeling happy somehow seemed to dishonor my son. How can I be happy? If the intense pain diminishes, does it mean my memory of him is diminishing too?

Sometimes I had to set *very* small daily objectives, such as simply remembering to breathe. That task was all I focused on, and I made it through the day. Even in my turmoil, this tiny win changed my mood and gave me strength to reach the next step. I've been guilty of setting lofty goals for myself and then falling short, and didn't want to add the internal struggle of fighting that *I can't* self-image while also grieving.

Another unexpectedly effective tool for healing was journaling, bringing clarity to all the jumbled thoughts I couldn't or didn't want to deal with as they poured onto a page. I grouped my experiences into two categories. One holds the situations that, although difficult, can be easily adjusted. I call this category variable challenges. For example, the loss of a job could mean learning new skills to obtain another. Or a divorce forces you out of your home, and you find new living accommodations. The adjustment may seem beyond solution, but finding a different path is clearly achievable.

The second group I labeled as static challenges: permanent situations that require discovery of an entirely alternate path. The loss of a child fits here. Or the loss of a spouse, your sight, or a limb in combat or in an accident. A static challenge produces a result that cannot be changed. So, as I struggled with grief over my son's death, whenever I felt there was no escape, I pieced together short- and long-term goals to keep me focused. Even though it felt as though the mountain was insurmountable, the invaluable lessons I had learned from creating unique ways to teach my son allowed me to devise novel approaches to find my new ways forward.

As my grief continued, there were chasms of reality in which I tried to reconcile the life I had once imagined and the one it had become. Finally, I realized that with all my expectations shattered, I was leading a life I could *never* have imagined. I determined I had three choices: 1) self-improvement, 2) status quo, and 3) self-destruction. Self-destruction was not an option. Although seeing no light at the end of the tunnel and wishing I could disappear, those I love depended on me, and I am not one to let them down. But the status quo was certainly not working either. Living in a fog of sadness was a miserable existence. Needing a to-do list to remember to breathe and eat was not sustainable. My only choice was self-improvement.

What I know now is that the path chosen determines the energy I extend to others. The well-known saying *misery loves company* comes to mind. As I navigated this self-improvement plan, the energy I projected gradually changed. I felt others being drawn to my energy of hope as my sadness dissipated. And as their positive energy expanded mine, it allowed more growth and possibility for me.

The eternal optimist in the core of my being knows that, just as a cracked sidewalk can allow the tiny amount of nourishment needed to grow a solitary dandelion, so can a hole in my soul allow healing to enter. My grief-filled life has now turned to anxious anticipation of experiences I never imagined, allowing them to sprout and reignite my desire to live.

Eliza Poe is, and may always be, a wandering gypsy spirit seeking higher purpose and searching for her place in the universe. Her past experiences shape the course she charts now, fueled by the desire to help others find their way through whatever difficulty they may currently be facing. Being a mom to a child with special needs taught her the benefits of outside-the-box solutions, and she is forever thankful for those lessons. This chapter debuts a new focus of work, as she channels her capacity for innovation into encouragement for those who need a cheerful reminder and support to guide them on their own journey. Eliza is creating new avenues to reach those who seek inspiration and reassurance in their personal healing paths. She raised her three children in Madison County, Illinois, where she remains a lifelong resident.

Justine Wilson

Just One More Day

"Just one more day. Just get through one more day. Surely tomorrow will be better."

For months, this was the only thought that got me out of bed in the morning. After my car accident left me with permanent brain damage and epileptic seizures, I was forced to give up my independence, job, and even driving. I was devastated to start my life all over again. It didn't seem fair after all my efforts, working my way up to being a manager at a job I loved, living my own life in a two-bedroom apartment. I was embarrassed to be an adult who suddenly needed to be driven around and constantly checked on and questioned by the people around me, who were always on edge that I might have a seizure. My whole life suddenly came to a halt, and I was forced to rely on my parents once again.

The brain damage and seizures disrupted my short-term memory too. My family struggled to understand why I forgot things they told me, and why they often had to repeat communications multiple times before I remembered. I could tell it made them angry sometimes, but there was nothing I could do to fix it. I started playing memory games to "exercise" my brain, hoping it would help, but it never did. I often felt that I annoyed my family and was better off spending time alone.

After a seizure, I stayed in bed for days. An epileptic seizure feels like a full-body workout on steroids, so the next day every muscle in my body was sore, including in my hands and feet. My head hurt so badly I cried when I first woke up, and the headache usually continued the rest of that day, if not two or three more. These headaches were excruciating and debilitating; I couldn't move, couldn't eat, barely slept because sleep brought no relief from the pain, and I even struggled to drag myself to the bathroom. Often, I thought no reason was strong enough to ever get me out of bed again, that I could stay there forever and never face this new life again.

Yet somehow I was always able to convince myself to get up one more time, to fight for one more day.

Moving back in with my mom who had recently divorced for the fourth time, in my mid-twenties, was not how I envisioned my life, especially because I try to stay separated from my mom's relationship drama. I never know what to expect when my mom starts a new relationship, as for each new partner, husband, or girlfriend, it seems my mom changes who she wants to be and expects me to change with her. When she was married to a pastor, we went to church every Sunday and lived the perfect Christian life. Now she practices witchcraft and has denounced the Christian faith.

Living with mom, I have always felt invisible. As her interests changed, I couldn't keep up, stay aligned with her interests. That dynamic strained our relationship, especially as my seizures got worse and I relied on the help of my family more and more. I often felt I was a burden to my mom and that she didn't want me around. And there was reality behind those feelings. I recently learned that Mom confided in one of my siblings during this time that she "didn't want to take care of a sick kid." But at the time I had nowhere else to turn.

Because of my memory loss, I also struggled with my mom's version of reality. She convinced me that I didn't remember things correctly or had done or said things I never had. I began to write myself small notes and send myself text messages, because I thought I was going crazy or that my memory was getting worse.

In 2019, I hit rock bottom and felt utterly defeated. No matter how much I tried to stay out of my mom's hair by finding other rides and getting help from my friends and siblings whenever possible, hoping to prove my independence and capabilities despite my frequent seizures, I never felt good enough. Trapped in the life I was living, I was just too exhausted to keep trying. Always going out of my way to make others happy even when it hurt me, I still felt invisible, and believed no one would notice if I was gone. Tired of perpetually falling short of my mom's expectations and feeling insufficient, I chose the only exit from pain I could see. I tried to take my own life.

My boyfriend at the time found me on the floor covered in blood and called 911. I cried when the EMTs arrived because I knew they would keep me alive, and I couldn't stop thinking "I hope my mom doesn't find out." I couldn't bear to see that look of disappointment in her eyes anymore.

After my short stint in the hospital psych ward, I was released to go home. I knew then that something had to change, and that day I decided I would never again let someone make me feel worthless or dependent. It was time to take back control of my life and start fighting for myself. The first step I took toward independence and self-worth was finding a fulfilling job, something to give me a purpose, and a reason to get up in the morning. So, I looked at online job possibilities—anything I could manage despite my health issues. I forced myself to update my resume, apply for jobs, and risk getting turned down. As challenging as those logistics proved, I also had to fight that voice in the back of my head telling me I would never again be successful in the employed world. Some days that voice was loud, but I just kept telling myself, *If I don't try, nothing will ever get better.*

After a hard grind of filling out job applications, dozens of interviews, and constant rejections, I was ready to give up. I was ready to condemn myself to a life of nothingness and feelings of worthlessness, when God sent me a savior. Virginia Muzquiz, Founder and CEO of Master Connectors, and Executive Director of BNI Mid America, decided to take a chance on me and hired me as her assistant. I finally had a reason to get up and get dressed in the morning. This job was my first step to reclaiming control of my life. Virginia mentored me and taught me about the world of entrepreneurship. Through my work with her, I met new people, made lifelong friends, and learned there were thousands of business owners out there who started with nothing, an idea that altered the entire trajectory of my life.

Working with Virginia I began to feel normal again. I was always learning something new and applying what I learned to my work. I discovered that under all the negative self-talk, I had a fire that was burning to do something great and become someone great. So, one small step at a time, I motivated myself to always be better than the day before.

After enduring seizures for nearly a decade, I confronted a critical decision when my medication failed to control my condition. Now I faced a life-altering decision: choosing a life of dependency with the full return of my seizures, or brain surgery. With no guarantees for the surgery's success, I felt trapped once again. I couldn't bear the thought of spending the rest of my life reliant on other people, and never regaining my independence. But having a piece of my brain removed without the guarantee it would end my seizures was terrifying and soul crushing. I felt it was a lose-lose choice and I was going to fall back into the pit of self-hate no matter which option I chose. This surgery was my first, and I was more scared than I had ever been. I had no idea what to expect, or what could go wrong. But I tried to stay hopeful. If the surgery worked, it meant no more seizures, no more headaches, and no more days spent in bed in agonizing pain. It meant I could finally drive again and get my life back! And all those possibilities were worth the risk.

Opting for surgery, I braced myself for a grueling recovery, and the aftermath *was* excruciating. For weeks I did nothing but sleep. Every movement hurt, and every time I stood up I thought my head would explode; the pain was relentless. I am thankful my sisters helped with my recovery, bringing me food and helping me to the bathroom. Without them, I don't know what I would've done.

As I slowly healed and started returning to my daily activities, I still struggled for months with a cognitive fog. Once again, my poor health put a strain on my relationship with my mom. I was moving slowly and thinking much more slowly than normal, and she didn't seem to have *that* much time for me.

During the surgery, they removed the visual memory part of my brain. Therefore, I can no longer remember what things look like, or directions to anywhere, not until I've repeated them enough for them to be rooted in my long-term memory. For the first year, I was often frustrated with myself for forgetting things, and for my slow thoughts. I was angry and scared that my memory was going to be permanently damaged, but there was a light at the end of the tunnel. Even if my brain never regained 100 percent functionality, this upgrade offered more control over my life, and I believed I could push through the last of this arduous journey to regain my independence. One step at a time, just one day at a time, I got better … a little better every day. Until finally I had the mental strength and the courage to open my own business, to start using all the skills I had learned despite my disability.

As I look back on my life, all the pain, anger, hurt, and defeat I fought through, I can now see the bigger picture. Although there will always be aspects of life I cannot control, I now know that I believe in myself, and I focus on what I can control.

I am living a self-governed life. I am the one who decides how I live. Looking ahead, I face the future with renewed hope and unwavering resolve. If I could overcome *those* trials, I am confident that I can conquer anything that comes my way.

Justine Wilson, a native of St. Louis, Missouri, and the second child of ten, embarked on a global journey with her family, initially as a military brat and later as a Christian missionary. Settling in the jungles of Peru in the early 2000s, she and her family embraced the Spanish language and warmly welcomed two Peruvian siblings into the family. Overcoming life-threatening epilepsy, Justine underwent successful brain surgery in 2020, igniting a newfound excitement for the future. With a wealth of experience gained from five enriching years under Virginia Muzquiz's mentorship, Justine honed her expertise in podcast management and marketing. Now, as the CEO of Premier Podcast Promotions, she offers tailored podcast management services, leveraging her skills to nurture her clients' businesses.

Tammy Egelhoff

Toto, We Aren't in Kansas Anymore!

For much of my life, I ignored the warning signs of approaching funnel clouds and allowed myself to be swept up by the tornadoes of life, leaving me vulnerable to turbulent winds. This pattern continued until the day I was jolted awake, utterly unprepared for the danger and treachery that lay ahead. All the while, I had no idea that I possessed a pair of red slippers, just like Dorothy in *The Wizard of Oz*, which I could click together to finally find my way back home.

Like Dorothy's, my journey along the yellow brick road was also full of uncertainty, fear, and doubt. I had no idea what had happened or how I got so far away from home. This particular tornado in my life came out of nowhere. I could not have predicted the price to return home from where I landed.

Life lessons teach us many things when we are faced with walking an unexpected path. Sometimes you are being celebrated as a hero for helping the Munchkins in your life, and other times you become the target of the Wicked Witches. And I had multiple such witches in my life, not just one. It takes a tremendous amount of courage to take the first step toward finding "the wizard," and the journey is better when you walk with others.

On my road to see the wizard, I discovered many things. One of my biggest discoveries was the wizard was neither the powerful wizard, as first seen in *The Wizard of Oz*, nor the kindly man behind that fire and smoke. Instead the wizard in my life was someone who proved he could not be trusted and could not be looked up to, who left me feeling betrayed and manipulated. This ultimate betrayal left me feeling unworthy, unvalued, and without my voice.

I am certain we've all known wizards in our lives, who had mystical powers and answers, and who exerted a certain level of control and influence over us. Other times, we might have been faced with moments when we wanted to turn our heads away and ignore what was behind that curtain. In those moments, I learned awareness is both a blessing and a curse. I had pushed through years of unthinkable obstacles to finally reach that pinnacle of self-awareness, only to see what I never wanted to see. How exceedingly difficult it is, not only to embrace that truth but to have the courage to walk away from everything I believed or perhaps wanted to believe. Trust had been broken not only with the wizards but also with myself.

What can I do when I can no longer *unsee* the truth? There is a fine line between influence and manipulation, and that fine line is intention. I found myself questioning the intentions of the wizards in my life. Perhaps some do have a good heart, believing their way is the only way that life should be lived. They believe their intentions to be good for those who enter Emerald City. My understanding of intention is that it is the fine line between influence and manipulation, which gave me the ability to see the lies and deception of the wizards. And in that moment, everything changed. In that moment, I wanted to start living instead of merely surviving.

At this time in my life, the biggest storm of all blew in as someone demanded I betray my soul. Although I felt at first that I was standing alone, my inner child was still there inside of me, begging me to finally take that stand. The stand to stop the manipulation, to get up off that floor, stand tall, and firmly say "*No*, not this time!" For me, this was the pivotal moment, when I knew I needed to stop betraying myself and instead honor my soul.

So I ripped down the wizard's curtain of manipulation and flipped the script. I asked myself and my inner child what she wanted. When I allowed myself to begin the journey of healing, I began to learn how to embrace the darkness that had shadowed, denied, and shaped my life. Once I finally realized that I was worthy of love, compassion, and grace, the tornadic winds started to die down. I learned I can't heal what I hide, what I ignore, what I cover, or what I avoid.

Now I recognized how seriously messed up, how insane my "wizard" had been, as all the while I was made to believe I was the delusional one. I realized this is no way to live, and so my journey down the yellow brick road began.

My healing journey sent me on a personal quest to meet my authentic identity and also to find my missing pieces. I gained personal development along the way with the help of the friends I encountered, starting with my wellness coach. Much like the Cowardly Lion, she taught me the importance of courage. By facing my fears, acknowledging my vulnerabilities, and doing what's right for my soul, I, too, can develop and have courage.

The next friend along the way was my spiritual advisor and Reiki master. Much like the Tin Man in Oz, she taught me that love does truly exist, and that learning to allow and balance all my emotions was true wealth, leading me back to find and heal my soul.

Another friend along the way was my mindset coach, who I liken to the Scarecrow. The Scarecrow showed me a different way of thinking and provided tools to allow me to see things in a much different, positive light. I learned to stop overthinking and second-guessing, to trust myself, my thoughts, and my decisions.

I took a gigantic leap of faith in beginning my wellness transformation, which led me to spiritual alchemy and a refining transformation through mindset development. Each of these healing modalities created a safe space that I had never encountered before. I expanded all my tools, understanding that in that safe space, there would be no judgment.

One last character in my story, who I liken to Glinda the Good Witch, is God. I now understand and embrace God's love for me, knowing it has always been unconditional, and directly tied to my belief in my self-worth and value. My hope is to now pass along to future generations the wisdom and invaluable life lessons discovered along my path.

I'll always be a work in progress, yet that will never stop me from regifting these transformational gifts I have learned along the way, always choosing progress over perfection. I believe we all possess inner magic that I like to call our ruby-red slippers. When activated, they illuminate a bright light that leads back home. I have them, you have them, and Dorothy had them too. Dorothy, if it feels like it's been a long road, maybe it's time to click those heels and come home.

Tammy Egelhoff is an intuitive and gifted spiritual alchemist, who is now changing the lineage for future generations. Making the personal quest to meet her authentic identity, Tammy embraced powerful modalities to achieve deep healing and transformation. The road map to complete wellness and wholeness now in hand, Tammy is grateful for God and her sister for intentionally causing her to cross paths with spiritual alchemy, knowing it freed her of the unrefined parts that needed healing: the lost identity and limiting beliefs, but, most importantly, forever freeing her soul. Tammy knows these transformational gifts, empowerment, and healing modalities will help others and has invested in her personal development by becoming a certified Reiki practitioner, neuro-linguistic programming (NLP) practitioner, and a health and wellness coach. Tammy is also one of the proud authors in *Perfectly I'Mperfect*, which became a #1 International Bestselling Book. She writes this chapter in loving memory of Kim Leann Bader. Thanks for the beautiful journey, Kim.

Andrea Allen

Awakenings

It's the end of another day. Once again, I have been counting down the hours to bed. I'm exhausted, hiding my depression, feeling like a failure as a mom because I can barely focus on what my five-year-old daughter is saying. My eight-year-old son is playing the drums, my two-year-old son is crying. I know my six-month-old baby girl needs to be changed. But I can't even snap up her sleeper because my hands are so inflamed. I am stumbling through every day like a sleepwalker because I have hidden my problems so well, I always feel alone. Unfortunately, I often *am* alone because my husband's work schedule as a UPS driver gives him just enough time to work and sleep.

How It Started

Shortly after the birth of my fourth child, I woke up to my body failing me. I felt like a voodoo doll filled with pins, on fire. I had always been relatively healthy, an athlete when I was younger. I lived a normal, active life until Leilani was born. What followed was months of medical visits, test after test, and numerous doctors who often left me feeling I wasn't being heard. Finally, I found a physician who seemed sympathetic and found a diagnosis. I was relieved to hear a name for my chronic pain and fatigue, although I had no idea what an autoimmune disease was. I believed that because we had a diagnosis, there would be a solution and I could finally wake up from this nightmare and begin living again.

But even in her kindness, the doctor's only solution was to eat better and get more rest. Ha! All I *wanted* to do was sleep. But chasing four kids, holding a part-time job, and having a spouse who was rarely available to help, I barely had time for a coherent thought or two each day. *How can I plan and prepare healthy meals?* I wondered.

Nothing changed for six years, though, until an ill-fated family hike. My enthusiastic husband wanted the whole family to hike a trail straight up a mountain in Weld, Maine. At the time, I could barely walk on level grass, so I have no idea why we thought I could trek up this steep, rocky trail with a section called Fat Man's Misery. I had just decided I was going to bull my way through with all four kids, even with the youngest only six years old. No problem! But the reality was that, for years, I'd not gotten down onto or up off the floor without help.

Less than half a mile in, there were rocks everywhere and all the tiny muscles in my feet were screaming in anguish. Straight ahead was a dreaded, narrow precipice of rock to navigate, using bars to pull ourselves through, like threading a needle with our bodies. Suddenly, I realized that I possessed neither the hand nor upper-body strength to accomplish this passage.

This is where I stopped and simply bawled, humiliated that I was losing control in front of my sister-in-law and her husband, who were bringing up the rear with me in tow. I hated crying or being out of control in front of others. I was so angry at my husband, angry at myself, and embarrassed that I *couldn't*. I was angry at my body that betrayed and failed me now at every turn.

I watched my four kids hopping from rock to rock on a grand adventure, like a bunch of billy goats. I was thirty-eight years old and felt like eighty-eight. I wanted so badly to be the fun mom who could jump up and do everything my kids did, but I couldn't keep up with them. I wanted ... no, I *needed* to be the woman I'm supposed to be: healthy, vibrant, creative.

When the tears wore me out and washed out all the anger, clarity began to form in my heart and mind. I needed a change and knew I would have to find it on my own, knew I could find my own solutions. I vowed to take control of what I *could* control.

Awakening #1: Control the Controllable!

In this disease-ridden journey, so far, my circumstances had controlled me. Always tired, I had little brain capacity for the hundreds of daily decisions required to run my household. Fighting depression, all I wanted to do was sleep until I could wake up and feel normal again. I felt like a fraud leading worship at church and pretending everything was OK when it definitely was not. In fact, I couldn't even clap my hands in praise because opening them fully was impossible. All the hiding, the pretending that everything was OK—that I was OK—drained what energy I did have and left me feeling spent like a dead battery.

My first "control the controllables" decision was to take some pressure off my joints by dropping weight. A friend and her husband had recently lost more than 150 pounds together, so I called her and said, "Whatever you did, I need that. Count me in!" I had no idea that this conversation would forever alter my life.

In August 2012, I began working with my new health coach and following a structured nutritional plan. I was so tired and really needed someone to spell out the plan plainly, making it easy for me to follow. After only eight days, I woke up and wept at the realization that I had just slept through the night for the first time in six years!

What was going on? This wasn't expected! I wasn't throbbing in constant pain. I had new energy. I wasn't calculating the hours to survive until bedtime, and my children were so happy to have an energetic mom. I felt like a portion of my brain had been rebooted like a computer, and that I was working with more gigabytes. I started having whole, continuous thoughts again. I'm awake! I'm *cured*! Or so I thought . . .

By 2013, I had transitioned from client to coach. I didn't want others to live in the prison of pain I had inhabited for so long. Reaching out to help others who felt stuck in their health, I began my coaching from the mindset, "I've got this figured out. What I used to eat was the cause of all my problems!" *Wrong!*

One day as I stood in my kitchen, coaching a client on the phone, I glanced over and saw a reflection of me eating a handful of chocolate chips. I suddenly realized, "I've still got some work to do."

Obviously, there is more to overall health than choosing nutritious food to fuel my body. When did this mindless nighttime eating begin again? A familiar pattern, yes, but not one I'd fallen into for the last twelve months. Some habits and patterns of behaviors clearly no longer served me, but while I found it easy to control the externals—like what food I bought and kept in the house—I knew my struggle to shift the internal required some changes in my thoughts and my identity.

Awakening #2: Change of Mindset

During this season, I began to walk our back-country roads while listening to Mindset/Performance Coach Ed Mylett and Financial Coach Robert Kiyosaki. Together, they created a university of my mind, one step at a time. As I endeavored to challenge my body, I also asked my mind to try hard things. I completed a twenty-eight-mile hike for the Make-A-Wish Foundation® and then completed a mini marathon.

Changing my daily reading matter to the writings of personal development leaders filled my mind with the enriching thoughts of authors like James Clear, Brené Brown, Bob Goff, and Stephen Covey. At the same time, to eliminate what no longer aligned with the future I desired, I began to say *no*. If a request for my time didn't serve my family or my business or personal growth, a new filter delivered an easy no. This boundary was new and exciting to me and lessened my emotional fatigue.

A few years later, a close friend shared that her therapist had asked her the question "What do you need right now?" Normally, I don't like big, esoteric questions. To my surprise, this one reverberated in my heart and mind and threw me into a tailspin. Unsure about this apparently crazy reaction, I began to pray for guidance. The Holy Spirit replied very plainly, "When are you going to stop seeing yourself as a victim? You have an amazing life!" I broke down and sobbed at this realization, and peace rushed in like a river flooding my heart with joy, appreciation, and contentment for the first time in a long time.

Awakening #3: Life Progress Is Marked by Growth!

Before this moment, my perception that I was never good enough in the eyes of my mother, my husband, and my kids was a self-imposed punishment. Suddenly, I saw life from a new perspective: I am good enough! I am loved! My interactions with my children and my spouse became more lighthearted. I didn't assume every misunderstanding was my fault. When drama or crisis arose, I practiced curiosity, pulling back the need to control or judge. I began to look with eyes of empathy that could see why the person across from me might be feeling some kind of way.

Soon, I no longer felt the need to respond to or correct family members' points of view. Letting go of that form of drama was transformational because it was my particular drug of choice. I felt I had dropped a rucksack full of rocks I hadn't known I was carrying.

How It's Going

I still have to *choose* every day not to fall back into that drama, and it's not always easy because drama carries a certain adrenaline rush. I am a bit embarrassed that I sometimes miss the social aspect of choosing sides in a dramatic argument because, when someone took my side, I felt I belonged. Even though I often cast someone I loved as the villain, this familiar path was easy to fall back to. Although also painful, *the familiar* feels less lonely than the path of the new.

There will be more shifts, more revelations, and more work to do. But I will pursue discovery and keep finding my tribe. Now, I seek out the people who support my journey. And I hope and pray that as long as I live, I will keep choosing the path of the new.

Andrea Allen is a dynamic certified health coach, speaker, and business leader who merges her passion for wellness with a zeal for inspiring others. With a heart set on holistic health, she empowers individuals to embrace vitality through her coaching and motivational talks that focus on battling autoimmune and inflammatory conditions. Andrea is dedicated to building a community of women who aspire to step into their God-given gifts and callings, fostering empowerment and finding the courage to flourish. Beyond work, she finds solace in the great outdoors, where hiking trails beckon and pickleball courts await her energetic spirit. Andrea's zest for travel fuels her exploration of new cultures and landscapes, enriching her perspective and igniting more wanderlust. As a multifaceted professional and avid adventurer, Andrea embodies a life where wellness, adventure, and inspiration intertwine harmoniously for a positive impact on others.

Derlene Hirtz

Becoming The Woman in The Mirror

"You are right on time."

Those were the words my spiritual director spoke fifteen years ago as I sat in her office full of anxiety and a great sadness I could not get past. I did not even know why I was so sad. As we had worked together over a couple of months, I kept asking the same questions: What is love? What is my true purpose?

"Right on time?" I asked, both amused and curious.

"Yes," Barb replied.

She knew I was familiar with music and used that metaphor to explain how life offers a certain rhythm and that I was in a cycle of a repeat bar. In music, a repeat bar means you repeat that section of music as many times as indicated. I was repeatedly playing the same music in my mind and expecting a different melody. Sigmund Freud calls that the definition of insanity: doing the same thing over and over and expecting different results.

Working with Barb was my first step to escape that repeat bar.

What brought me to her office was *The Woman in The Mirror*. Putting on my makeup one morning, I didn't recognize the person staring back at me. Sure, physically it was me, just a bit older with well-earned wrinkles outlining my eyes, and my once auburn hair now graying. But as I leaned in and peered deeper into my hazel-green eyes, a hollow note boomed in the depths of my soul: "Who am I, really?" I thought about how I'd heard the eyes are the windows to the soul. I leaned in to take a closer look. Staring back at me were once-sparkling eyes that now looked sad, lost, hopeless, lifeless. When had the mischievous twinkle disappeared?

All that I've learned over these past ten years has allowed me to answer those questions, and more, and to recapture The Woman in The Mirror.

In this short story, I share one of my greatest learnings: choice is powerful, and suffering is optional.

We create as we speak and think, and my thoughts and words brought about immense personal suffering. I have discovered suffering is created three different ways: the illusion to control, demanding things be different, and arguing with what is.

I found myself in a toxic work environment. The truth is that I took that job on 100 percent ego and knew within twenty-four hours I didn't belong there, yet I stayed for six and a half years. I was working at a church and naively believed that meant I was working for God. In no time at all, I realized I was working for a man who had his own agenda. I clearly see now that I was trying to control an environment I had very little control over.

I believed if I worked hard, was kinder, and showed more interest, my toxic work environment would somehow be different. The more I tried to make positive changes, the more unhappy I became.

I created more personal suffering by reasoning with myself that it *would* be different. I would be accepted because I mattered. My reality was life at work only got more self-defeating the harder I tried.

I caused myself an immense amount of suffering. Understanding that people do the best they can with the tools they have, I chose to learn new tools that allowed me to move forward. The toxic work environment was a great learning experience. I am grateful I had the experience because it led me to seek The Woman in The Mirror.

Up to this point in my life, I prided myself on being a do-it-yourself kind of gal, always telling myself I could handle anything life brought my way. That was my ego talking, and I learned the number one person I lie to is myself. I had to admit I'd been lying to myself for many, many years as a cover for all my insecurities.

I was exhausted from listening to the Old Nag ... you know, the voice in my head. (Like the one in your head that just responded, "I don't have a voice in my head." That one.) The Old Nag follows me around wherever I go, constantly reminding me of my imperfections, that I am dumb, have limitations, and that other people are better than me.

Barb, my new spiritual director, was the first person who created a safe place for me to question who I am, what I wanted, and how I could make changes in my life that would allow me to discover my purpose and calling. I spent most of my time with Barb reflecting on my life and patterns, and building a new foundation as I got to know The Woman in The Mirror.

I began asking myself, "Who am I, really?" How had I gotten to this place, so far from the happy mom, wife, employee, and friend I once was? Immediately, the Old Nag stepped in and reminded me in her sassy, authoritative voice, "Yes, how *did* this happen? You are a very fortunate woman, with a man who loves you, great kids, friends who adore you, and your parents are still healthy." The Nag took one last shot at my sense of worth, tossing my job at a church into my face, adding, "You're *working for God* for heaven's sake! Get it together, girl!"

And down the slippery slope of shaming and beating myself up I slid, hitting that repeat bar again and again. The Woman in The Mirror, exhausted from years of being *the other woman* to the Old Nag, pleaded with me to free her.

One night I came home from work, and my husband, Steve, was out of town. I felt I was in a scene from a movie. It was dark outside, and I knew I would be walking into an empty house. In this movie scene, I saw the director had placed an angel on one shoulder and the devil on the other. Their conversation was very spirited!

Angel: "Derlene, you should not go home tonight. You are in no state of mind to be home alone. You need to go to Cathy's house and talk to her."

Devil: "Well, how ridiculous is that going to be? Showing up at her house saying a voice in your head told you to come to her house instead of your own?"

Angel: "That's what friends are for, and Cathy is your best friend."

Devil: "Well, go ahead. Go to her house and look like a fool. You will be embarrassed, and she will probably take you to the psych ward."

OK, Devil, you and your sidekick, Pride, win! I went home and completely lost myself, crying and screaming, even begging and bartering with God.

A couple of years after meeting Barb, my angel in real life, in human form, I found myself in a training program for neuro-linguistic programming, or NLP. My understanding of NLP is as a set of tools to help us better understand how we think, communicate, and build relationships, both with ourselves and with others. This training launched my further study of and obsession with mindset, success, and excellence.

I came to NLP via another horrible fight with the Old Nag. She had convinced me my life was so miserable that I wanted to die because I would forever be buried under the misery I called my life. Silencing the Nag for a moment, I thought to myself, "OMG! Here I go again!" This time, a series of angel/devil conversations ended differently; the angel won!

I picked up the phone, called best friend Stacey, and never looked back … except to use the past as a learning opportunity to move forward. I quit the job, started two businesses, and now get to spend my days helping others journey into their most successful lives. What could be better than that?

Today, when I see The Woman in The Mirror, I see a vibrant, smart, kind woman staring back at me. When life throws me curves, I assess whether I am choosing to suffer and if I can take action toward a different choice.

The Woman in The Mirror has been there all along. I simply had to journey deeply into my inner self to find *me* again. Now, I am full of energy and allow my Light to shine for all to see. No longer listening to the Nag, the Devil, and his sidekick Pride, or any of the human naysayers I meet, I am inviting others to join me. Together, our Light can transform the world. Most exciting in my "new" reflection in the mirror is the sparkle back in my eyes. My sparkle has returned because I know my life is what I create it to be. The Woman in The Mirror is just waiting her instructions to make that happen. She was there all along.

Derlene Hirtz works with entrepreneurs and sales professionals who are ready to transform their approach to success, as CEO (Chief Empowerment Officer) of You Empowered Services (YES). She is a seasoned mindset strategist and leader, with years of experience coaching and training clients to break through barriers that hinder their success. Derlene believes the foundation of a successful business lies in the mindset of its leader. She approaches her coaching and training with a passion to see others succeed.

At its core, YES is dedicated to helping individuals harness a success-focused mindset and helping them build profitable, purposeful, and productive businesses. YES offers one-on-one coaching, masterminds, and certification training in neuro-linguistic programming (NLP), all to address the unique challenges faced by today's business climate. Whether you seek to refine your business strategy, increase sales effectiveness, or cultivate a leadership style that inspires, Derlene's *YES!* is your success solution.

Sheila Riggs

Becoming My Own Advocate

Not another ear infection … Not another round of antibiotics … How can I be so sick so often? The physician assistant is attentive and considerate, and I really like her. She says she doesn't actually *see* anything, but according to my chart I get these infections so often, she thinks my body must recognize I'm getting one before its visible. How is that even possible?

At this point, I've seen five medical professionals in five years. The doctors, nurse practitioners, and physician assistants are all sympathetic to my woes and tell me to "hang in there." I'm just predisposed to getting this type of infection, they say. They order hearing and balance tests over the years, which all have great results; I'm not dizzy, and I have perfect hearing. *What else could that be* except an ear infection, right? I take my prescription slips and head to the pharmacy … again.

At the start of those five years, I heard a *whooh*-ing sound in my right ear. Do you know what an ultrasound for a baby's heartbeat sounds like? Yep, exactly like that. *Whooh. Whooh. Whooh.* At first the sound came and went; it wasn't constant and was really faint, like a background noise. I told friends, who suggested it was just tinnitus. My husband definitely thought so, and he's a drummer who didn't protect his ears. Nobody explained what tinnitus sounds like: high-pitched squeals that make it hard to hear certain pitches. But my experience was that I had perfect hearing ... and a sound in my head I couldn't make anyone understand.

Our family rarely has any medical needs, thankfully. But as a result, I don't know how to talk to these professionals who I assume are the experts. Who am I to question what they say? I feel that I'm complaining too much, so I try to ignore this heartbeat in my head. I don't want to be a bother to these doctors who probably think I'm crazy by now or just want meds. Our insurance coverage is disgraceful, and my family can't afford my "issues."

After years of this back-and-forth, a friend suggests I see an ear, nose, and throat specialist (ENT) for another opinion. Ugh ... That requires seeing my primary care doctor and telling him "I don't trust your care and want to see someone else." But I find the courage to do it, and he writes the referral for an ENT. Months later I finally see this specialist ... and he sends me for hearing and balance tests. I pass them—yet again—with flying colors. Back I go to his office for yet another co-pay and another round of antibiotics for an ear infection that I'm no longer sure I have.

As I wait for my follow-up appointment, I visit a friend whose son needs an in-home health care nurse. The nurse is there, and my friend suggests I tell her what I'm going through. I relay the whole story, feeling like I'm *really* being a baby about some elusive "sound in my head." The nurse says she doesn't think I'm crazy at all. In fact, she used to work for a practice where one patient had a vein lying against her eardrum, so she was hearing the same thing! She suggested I ask the ENT for an MRI.

No doctor had ordered this test. I couldn't believe it! Finally! A possible solution!

At my next appointment, I share this conversation with the doctor, but he replies, "I don't know what you have but that's not it." In the moment, I envision him patting me on the head like a silly little girl who is asking for dessert before dinner. My mental ear takes in the meaning: *Of course you can't have dessert before dinner! I can't even believe you'd ask such a silly question! Oh, and, by the way, that female nurse who told you to ask this doesn't know what she's talking about either.*

But I can't accept that anymore. The *whooh, whooh, whooh* in my head keeps getting louder, and I can no longer accept "I don't know what you have, but that's not it" as my final answer. Sitting in his exam room, growing more frustrated as the volume rises—*Whooh! Whooh!*—and about to cry ... I suddenly realize that it *is* usually louder when I'm stressed. I need results! There must be a better remedy!

When I asked for the MRI to absolutely rule out this possibility, he said no. Hearing him shoot down a potential solution, I asked why not. And *he* told *me* that it's an expensive procedure that *I don't want to pay for*. I was stunned ... *shocked* that he thought he could presume to know what I wanted. Finally, I found the courage to push back. "I have paid co-pays for expensive tests for five years now with no diagnosis. If the MRI is that expensive, maybe my insurance will finally pay for *something!*" He huffed, "Fine!" and left the room.

A few days after the MRI, this ENT leaves me a voicemail: "It's not what you thought it was. It's much worse. Someone will be in touch."

Referred to a surgeon at a highly respected hospital in the next state, I'm told I have a condition called Chiari malformation. Essentially, some of my brain stem is bulging through the normal opening at the base of my skull, constricting the flow of spinal fluid. He tells me that usually Chiari is seen in babies born with spina bifida or people with head trauma, but neither applies to me. He recommends surgery that will sever one of the muscles that hold up my head, requiring four to six months of recovery while that muscle repairs itself. It's like his voice gets farther and farther away, and all I can think is, *"This can't be happening!"* Nine surgeons in the department are discussing how to proceed and will be in touch with more information.

I feel I don't have a choice; I must do this. I'm terrified and have no idea how my husband and kids will manage while I'm laid up, not working, unavailable for anything. With the noise a constant now, I can't sleep, I have terrible headaches, and I can't *think*! When I want to read, I've learned to push the little indentation under my ear to gain a few moments of silence. It's incredible to finally have some peace!

At my next appointment, I meet a different surgeon who explains that when the team reviewed my case, he asked to step in. Joking that he is "older than dirt," he tells me that he has read all the standard medical journals and now reads the obscure ones no one else has time for. He believes that I have a sigmoid sinus diverticulum and that if we eliminate that, the pressure in my head will cease and the Chiari will be relieved. This diagnosis (if true) means that a wayward piece of one carotid artery—we all have one on either side of the neck, carrying blood from the heart to the brain—found its way through a cavity in my skull *and is near my eardrum*! Oh, and he advises I stop pressing that little indentation because I'm cutting off blood flow to my brain. He says that it's a good thing none of my kids started a pillow fight because even a small blow to my head could make it burst and kill me instantly. I cry in relief when he puts the end of a stethoscope to my head and taps his finger in time to the *whooh*. He can hear what I hear!

I will be one of fewer than twenty people who've had surgery for this diagnosis, the doctor says, and the majority are obese, older men from outside the United States. He explains that, while risky, it is actually outpatient surgery. They will make an incision behind my ear to give access to my skull. After they compress the artery, they will repair the hole with a little "spackle" made from medical adhesive mixed with bone chips and bone dust from my skull. He says that unfortunately they cannot eliminate the bulge completely. It's a BandAid, not a fix, so I will likely have this surgery again at some point, but they don't know what they don't know.

Obviously, as I am here to write the story, the surgery was successful! I was told the observation area of the surgical suite was packed with intrigued medical professionals. The bigger success, though, is that my surgeon wrote a paper about it and doctors worldwide began more accurately diagnosing patients like me. A team of surgeons even began studying the repair procedure and created a new material that is better than my "spackle."

Eight years later, I began to hear that *whooh* again, so I called the surgeon's office immediately, and I got to be one of the first people to have this surgery a second time! It may not even be the last because they still did not have a permanent solution at that surgery. That's OK, too, because I'm not afraid anymore to stand up for myself and my right to be heard when something feels wrong. It would have been easy to let the *professionals* keep explaining away my complaints. It would have been less confrontational to say "OK" instead of insisting on continued testing of a different kind. It also would have been to my own detriment if I had just left that ENT's office, accepting his opinion. If it wasn't for my self-advocacy for help with my medical issue, I would not be here today. And I will continue to fight, unapologetically, for my own health.

Sheila Riggs is a wife of more than twenty-five years and a mother to four fabulous children and an incredible son-in-law. A Realtor on the Illinois side of the St. Louis–Metro market, she makes time for her family and friends not only because she loves them but because she has learned that we never know when our mortality will be tested. She's had hers "tested" four times. She loves educating her real estate clients and fellow agents on the systems, models, and tools that result in win-win home sales and purchases. Her Skyline Community Realty Team keeps growing and shining, even as she also volunteers in her local community to make her corner of the world a better place. In her playtime, Sheila loves being outdoors and strives to learn something new every day. People know her for her smile and her laugh because life is too short to live without them.

Ann Langston

From Shouting and Silence to Saving the Kids

I stepped out into the bright Tucson sun. It was 117 degrees and felt like a blow-dryer on max blowing from across the flight line. The aircraft I worked on were so hot I had to wear gloves to touch them. That scorching desert is where we met, where our story began.

Not sure if it was the desert sun or heat stroke, but we did everything fast. From meeting in the Air Force as we worked on the flight line to getting married only took us three months. A year later, both honorably discharged, our family had already grown with the addition of our first child. We had two more before number one reached four years of age. My husband's new job in civil service for the Air Force moved us back to the Midwest to be near our families when the kids were six, four, and two.

On fire like the desert heat, our life was a hot swirling wind, and nothing was easy. From the start, *nothing* about our relationship was healthy. Our only points of agreement were that we both fiercely loved our children and were hard-working and ambitious. That's where the similarities stopped.

He thrived on conflict and chaos. Peace at any price was my sole focus and became my survival instinct. There is a deep cost for allowing people to walk all over you in the name of peace: a lesson I had to learn and *still* struggle with daily. If I cleaned the entire house spotless but left one dish in the sink, that dish generated a confrontation. He was obsessive and very vocal in all his compulsions. A strong individual by nature, I found myself exhausted after birthing, nursing, and caring for three children, while also devoting big portions of my day preparing to tiptoe around him once he arrived home.

The conflict in our marriage grew. Nothing I did was right. His way was the only way. I couldn't have an opinion or contradict his ideas. He was cheery and upbeat with people outside our home, so everybody else *loved* him. He made sure to look perfect to anyone beyond the family, so my life seemed fantastic to outsiders. But at home, he took out his frustrations on those closest to him, our family. We were fighting in front of the children nonstop, without filters or discretion. It horrifies me to realize the conversations they must have heard.

The fireworks had to end.

The tipping point was when I caught him cheating, but my guilty truth is that I was relieved. I finally had an escape hatch from an extremely unhappy situation, and a valid reason for the rest of the world. I'm sad to realize now that the angry, demeaning words and emotional trauma weren't enough to justify leaving.

As soon as I decided to leave, I felt *free*.

The kids were ten, eight, and six when I filed for divorce, and it was finalized the next year. Proud to be an example for my kids, I showed them we can choose to stand up for ourselves and expect better treatment.

Now focused on healing the children and myself, my mantra became *I love my kids more, I love my kids more, I love my kids more*. Each time a new conflict required me to make a tough choice, those words rang in my head.

I Love My Kids More!

As in marriage, we didn't follow tradition when it came to being divorced and taking care of our kids. Conflict continued, and we still argued and disagreed over the phone, but we tried not to shout at each other in front of the kids. We each never spoke badly about the other to the kids. We agreed on this key point, knowing such behavior causes stress and long-term grief for kids, and robs them of their childhood. We may not have navigated the change perfectly, but we tried to minimize the post-divorce pain for the children.

My viewpoint never changed that, above all other concerns, they are *my* children. I am responsible for them, and I will do whatever I can to protect them. My role is to help them grow up as happy as possible, no matter what is going on with their father.

I didn't need to fan the flame … but I did feel strongly sometimes that I *hated* him. My grandmother taught me *We do not hate people*. I might dislike or disagree with them but never hate them. Well, that was tough for me, because at times I hated my ex, and that is a powerful feeling! That emotion rises above all logic.

I Hated Him!

So many emotions follow a divorce: hate, dislike, jealousy, grief, sadness, anger, shame … the list can be long. If you have divorced, you may have felt them all as you lost a life you thought you would get to live but no longer get to enjoy. I gave up what I thought was going to be the perfect life.

Now the dream, the fairy tale, is over. Of course I felt that I hated him … *sometimes*.

The Antidote to Hate

The antidote is to take responsibility for *my* actions. For every decision involving the children, I stop and think about the impact it will have on them. I was not going through a divorce by myself. They are going through it too!

Our Secret Sauce

My ex and I decided to follow some simple rules, easy to identify and harder to follow. For example, we remained flexible about drop-off and pick-up times. And if one kid wanted to spend time with one parent or the other, or just needed time *away* from one parent, we respected their decision and gave them the freedom to make that choice. We also agreed we would not confide in our children like best friends. Finally, we knew that we would all congregate together for events like graduations, birthdays, holidays, and weddings, so we made sure the kids never felt uncomfortable having both of us there.

My experience is now the foundation for a book about how parents' actions after a divorce affect their kids. The impact of these experiences is affecting generations to come. It does not matter if children were young or an adult when their parents divorced. How those parents handle it can change their children's lives forever.

To write my book, I interviewed my children—now thirty-two, thirty, and twenty-eight years old—before anyone else, and asked them to be brutally honest. I was pleasantly surprised at their consistent reaction of gratitude for removing them from a bad, argumentative, chaotic state and creating a life of peace and balance.

The hummingbird on this book cover is perfect for my story, as a symbol of adaptability because of their agility and speed, navigating life's challenges with grace and resilience. Also, we parents need to be able to pivot, and hummingbirds fly up, down, right, left, and even backward. These resilient, small birds fly farther than most, and are a symbol for how we could live our lives.

There is power in the hummingbird's story; they are a vision of hope. I created a vision board journal with hummingbirds hidden on the pages to spark joy when you find them. One of the ways I took back control of my life was with my vision board journal. I still read it every day and remember all of my *I am* statements: I am lovable, I am strong, I am capable, I am enough, I am happy, I love my life, and I love me.

I had found that my marriage was a battleground and saw that it wasn't good for our kids. The negativity didn't end, but the secret sauce that saved our kids was our mutual choice to keep that conflict private. I learned that divorce is not just about you, how you are feeling, or how you feel justified. No matter what happened to you.

One of the greatest lessons I learned was that words are powerful; so I am careful what I say, for my words will be remembered for a lifetime. My marriage started with extreme *shouting*. I was ashamed of my *silence* during the turbulent years. Finally, my life changed for the better when I made the commitment and gathered the strength and support to *save* my kids. I have always, and will always strive, to do what is best for my kids, for they are my joy and my world. They are the greatest gift I have ever been given, and I am grateful for knowing what amazing adults they have become.

Ann Langston, who publishes under the name Michelle Marie, is a single mother of three amazing adults and a grandmother of three incredible grandchildren. Writing under her *nom de plume*, using her middle name Michelle and her inspirational identical twin sister's middle name Marie, gives her the most freedom and joy to be who she is. Ann is the published author of *Pocket Vision*, the vision board journal that motivates you to think *big* in creating your vision for your life. In her professional life, she is a divorce coach who supports those affected by divorce, and she is a Missouri and Illinois Supreme Court–approved mediator while she continues her work as a mortgage lender, with more than twenty-two years' experience. Ann's latest book, coming out in 2024, gives the children of divorce a voice.

Layla Evans

Who Am I?

"Ouch!" I looked down at the rock that just hit the back of my head, dropping me to my knees. I looked up to see two older girls from my neighborhood pointing and laughing from the other side of my fenced-in front yard. "You stupid, ugly, white b*tch! You don't belong here! You smell as bad as your dumba** dog. We can't wait till you both die. Nobody here likes you." I didn't understand why they were being so mean, and I couldn't contain the tears rolling from my eyes. That only made their taunting worse. They grabbed more rocks and threw them at me as I ran away and went inside. "Go tell yo mama! She better not do nothing, or my brother gone come back and shoot all ya'll a**es." They ran away just as I got to the door.

"Layla Dawn! What did you do to your dress!? You haven't been outside more than twenty minutes and it's ruined! This is why I don't ever buy you anything! Why are you crying? You know what, I don't even care, go clean yourself up!" My mother's words chased me, too, as I frantically ran into the house. I guess when I fell to my knees, I landed in the mud.

A first grader with olive skin and curly dark hair, I lived with my Caucasian mother and grandparents in a not-so-accepting neighborhood. On this day, the whole family came over for Easter Sunday, and I was outside looking for Easter eggs with my dog, wearing this beautiful blue, lacy dress. I had been so excited to wear it because we didn't have a lot of money and I rarely got anything new such as clothes or toys. After some time, my mother came into the bathroom to help me clean my dress, and I was able to tell her what happened. She told me to stay away from those girls, not to worry about the things they said, and to go play in the back yard with the rest of my cousins.

I returned to the backyard where my cousins were, and something immediately felt off. The ones who would normally run up to me and want to play had been ignoring me all day: looking at me and then looking away as if I wasn't there. I asked my favorite cousin if she wanted to come play Barbies with me. She looked at me and seemed to be terrified to be seen talking to me. She said her mom told her she can't play with me anymore. My heart sank, my chest felt heavy. Every memory of us playing together raced through my mind. What could I have done to cause this?

Then her older sister came over and said, "You know mom said not to play with the little ni**er girl anymore. Get away from her before we get gross too." Just then, an older cousin who I really looked up to sauntered over. I was certain she was coming to make things right. Surely, there was some kind of mistake, and her first words seemed to confirm that. "She's not a ni**er" were the words that echoed like music in my soul. I didn't even know what that word was or meant but knew it could not be good if they weren't allowed to play with one. I was just so happy she had my back and things could go back to normal. Then she continued ...

"She's a *sand-ni**er*. They're worse. They hump camels and have fleas and lice. That's why we stay away from them. Our moms said we don't have to come over here anymore after today because it's too ghetto." They all three continued to point at, laugh at, and taunt me while I stood frozen in shock and disbelief. This loss hurt worse than the rock that had hit me moments earlier. I had never experienced this type of hurt before. It wasn't their words that I didn't even understand but the betrayal I felt, and for reasons I couldn't comprehend at such an early age. I didn't understand prejudice. I didn't think we were different. I didn't know why any of this was happening. I was so upset, I felt numb, unable to feel my body or react.

Something in my brain changed that day. The pain and confusion broke me. My best efforts to analyze and understand only left me more perplexed. I can't explain or describe the brokenness other than as a profound sense of loneliness and emptiness. I felt that everything I ever knew was wrong, and I truly had no one. I didn't say anything but just sat and watched their behavior in complete disbelief. Today, because of this early betrayal, I still struggle with personal relationships and have difficulty getting close to people.

Eventually, my mother came out and yelled at them. Then I heard more yelling inside between her and the other adults. Soon everyone left, and we didn't have many family gatherings after that. In fact, the only interaction I had with those cousins for years afterward was receiving a box of their hand-me-down clothes. I didn't want to wear them, but they were often the only choice.

Not long after that day in the backyard, at school in our first-grade recess, those older neighbor girls who threw rocks at me were there with some more of their friends. They started pulling my hair, slapping me, and calling me new racist names that were worse than the ones I heard from my cousins. I ran to tell the teacher, who yelled at me for tattling and said, "You're grown up enough to handle this situation on your own." The girls then physically carried me out of the teacher's sight and started kicking and punching me.

The creepy janitor intervened and hid me in the closet "for safety." When the bell rang, he wouldn't let me leave and became extremely inappropriate and predatory. He started to forcibly undress me and exposed himself. I managed to unlock the door and run away with my overalls half-off. When the principal found me in the hallway and asked why

I wasn't in class, the janitor ran up and interrupted before I could answer. He claimed that the older girls and I were trying to break into his space and destroy his equipment, and that he chased me out of his closet. The principal called my mother to the school and, shortly after, I was enrolled in a private school.

The private school might have been a blessing, except we were poor and everyone else was not. So, at six years of age, I'd been alienated from my family for not being white enough, alienated from my neighborhood friends for not being Black enough, and unable to make friends in grade school because I was not rich enough.

I spent the next several years trying to find someplace to fit in. When with my Black friends, I made racist jokes about my white family, listened to their music, and started dressing like them. When with my Caucasian family, I made racist jokes about my friends, my culture, and its history. I bullied and made fun of other kids who were less fortunate than me at school to shift attention from my shortcomings. I hung out with boys and made fun of girls because I couldn't find girlfriends who wouldn't judge me.

I spent the majority of my young life trying to be something I wasn't, just to fit in *somewhere*. I wanted so badly to feel welcomed but never really felt accepted, or that I *belonged*.

By the very young age of nine, I was depressed and using drugs and alcohol to numb all my feelings. I acted out my sense of complete isolation with many poor choices. Promiscuous and suicidal, I dropped out of school, pregnant before I turned eighteen.

My whole life changed the moment I saw the positive lines on the pregnancy test. First, I knew my life was no longer only about me but now included another life I was responsible for. Knowing my current situation was not the best, I clearly saw the need for changes. I vowed my baby would have the best life had to offer and wouldn't need to struggle or worry as I had.

So I immediately quit all drugs including alcohol, nicotine, and even caffeine. By my second trimester, I moved out of the bad neighborhood I lived in, and two months before my daughter was born, received my high school diploma. And I finally found an identity that felt like belonging. I was a mom. I was going to be the best mom I knew how to be. I wasn't always perfect, but d*mn did I try! I still do.

After living as a single mom for about ten years, I got engaged to my best friend and his two daughters. Our kids had always been best friends and couldn't have been happier to call themselves sisters. My Hope, Faith, and Justus are now twenty-four, sixteen, and twenty-one. The only problem with the mom identity is that kids grow up and then move away. While I'm so proud of their accomplishments, I am no longer needed as a full-time mom. Soon, I found myself trying once again to figure out who I am. Mom, wife, friend, manager, entrepreneur? Those are titles other people give me. Who am I?

I'm Layla. No, that's just a name. There are plenty of others out there. Who am I deep down? Neither white, black, nor any other color. Not a racist or a bully. I'm not a drug addict, reckless, rich, or poor, and I no longer strive to create myself as someone I'm not just to fit in. I don't crave the approval of others to authenticate my self-worth. I no longer care about the opinions or expectations of anyone outside of my household.

No, those old thoughts patterns and words from childhood don't define me, though they did shape me into who I am today. But they don't represent my journey to find growth and peace and happiness in my authenticity. Those ugly words are not the years I spent trying to figure out who I am to this world. It took me a long time to find the truest version of myself, and now I help others find theirs.

So, I ask again, who am I? I am loving and accepting. I'm forgiving and ever evolving. I am forever a student and a teacher. I am true to myself. I am living a purposeful, meaningful life, which I hope inspires others. I am love and expansion. I am perfectly imperfect. Who are you?

Layla Evans' Arabian father returned to his home country when she was only two years old, leaving her to be raised by her poverty-riddled Caucasian mother and grandparents in a predominantly African American neighborhood. In her professional life, she wears all the hats. She is a certified life coach at Layla Dawn Does Life, where she aspires to help others learn how to live life authentically and purposefully. A serial entrepreneur, voice actor at Layla's Voices, mermaid entertainer, and model, she won several titles as Ms. Missouri of the Monarch International Pageant, which focuses on inclusivity. As Siren Slayla, LLC she partners with and donates time to several nonprofit organizations and environmental institutions. As an independent travel agent, Layla also runs the Mermaid Division of Ambassador Travel and Cruises. She has three amazing adult children and loves to travel as often as possible.

Kay Pierson

Home

I swallowed hard at the lump in my throat and stared down at an untouched dinner plate. The slow-cooked tension and anxiety is a meal of its own. I'm no longer interested in the food in front of me. Every atom in my body screams to run. There is nowhere to go. I am home.

Pick up the fork and consume the situation.
In bed that night, my mind swam through problems I did not create and circumstances a child cannot change, searching for solutions. The exercise was soothing only because the alternative was to accept that I must wallow in a fishbowl of toxicity no one else was coming to clean. Why was everyone so angry? How can people say they love you in one moment and then speak hateful words the next? I never found those answers.

Truthfully, this could have been a Tuesday, Friday, Christmas, or my birthday; nights like these were not unusual. That environment was built brick by brick in daily incidents. A home and family filled with constant turmoil and plagued by hatred teaches hatred. It is that overwhelming feeling of being trapped, unable to escape the persistent negativity, that my story focuses on.

My childhood memories include a birthday party ending with my terrified friends and I pushing our full weight against my bedroom door as it shook with the blows of a family member attempting to break it down.

Another birthday dinner ended with hearing I looked like a "whore" in my senior photos. One Christmas an exceptionally burly family member screamed in my elderly great-grandmother's face, calling her a b*tch. I watched my grown sister being beaten naked for taking too long in the shower. I used to run my toe along a dent created when a barstool met the hardwood during another of these nights and reflect on the silent damage that lingers long after the chaos ends.

I am dented like that hardwood floor.

Gun threats, hidden guns, car-tracking devices, drug use, stalking, running to the neighbors' house for safety, cheating, addiction, lies, police, broken doors, busted phones, changed locks, divorce, vodka refilling chain-store coffee cups at eight in the morning, and screaming. So much screaming, yelling, and hate. None of this aggression was sourced by relatives my age. These were the adults in my life, to whom most children can turn to for safety. The unpredictability of these players fostered a silent internal panic at any family gathering.

When a home is condemned, it's torn down.

My eyes opened to the sun sneaking around the edges of the blackout curtains. The room was dim, and my pounding head replayed the night's events. The celebration of my eighteenth birthday had fallen into shambles with virtual daggers pointing my way. I have never felt more genuinely hated than that night.

I sat up and unwillingly swung my feet to the floor, pressing them into the shag rug. Staring into the mirror before me, facing myself, I dreaded yet again opening that bedroom door to face whoever and whatever waited on the other side.

I couldn't spend another night in this bed I did not make for myself. The exhausted girl staring back from the mirror was pleading for help. I broke. The frequent and familiar gut reaction to *run* finally won.

The trash bags stretched and burst as I filled them with the choicest life belongings of a teenage girl. Knowing the once-in-a-lifetime events lined up for the coming two months, I hastily filled these bags to satisfy those obligations. Work aprons, business wear for the national high school debate Tournament of Champions, a comfort flannel for my portfolio art showing, a cap and gown for graduation, and prom heels that punctured the thin wall of the trash bag. Finally, I slipped into the back closet and draped my sister's old prom dress over my shoulder. Then, trash bags in hand, I left.

Total home demolition is impossible from the inside.

I descended the stairs to my safe place. I had found refuge with some family members who had a history of being my saviors. I remembered a sentiment they'd shared years prior: "It is better to be *from* a broken home than *in* one." The concept of home changed for me over the next year. Home was the isolation of a basement. Home was where I could relax … no one tried to knock down that door. I find the inherent darkness of a basement calming to this day.

The treachery of the world happened out there, not within my four walls. I endured the attempts to regain some form of control over me. Destructive people will not let go easily of toys they enjoy playing with. Never once did I regret leaving, and my desire for distance only grew as these individuals continued to show me the truth of their character.

I don't believe I have to forgive, forget, or heal every broken relationship in my life. One of the hardest things I did was simply to let go, to choose myself, and to commit to that choice. I claimed the power to determine who is part of my world, family, life, and home.

For the first few months I chose that basement and its seclusion, uninterested in other humans and life altogether. I chose solitude until I fell in love at first sight with the sweetest of souls, divinely sent for me in that time of need.

Home became a four-legged friend with the most loving sparkle in his eyes, a puppy named Casper. His presence was the catalyst for learning that peace could come without complete isolation, and after so much time cutting the world out, I became more willing to let something new in. Casper is a testament to the healing power of unconditional love, and how it can inspire rebirth. We were a little family of two, in a basement.

Once the fear of the unknown has passed, demolition is complete, and the dust is settled, there is only one thing left to do.

Rebuild.

The bricks were heavy as I rebuilt home. Each one symbolized the people, opportunities, and places I allowed to fill my life, and I was careful to curate them for my true peace and happiness. For five years, who I wanted to be and who I did not want to be shaped every decision I made about my concept of home. I chose carefully, knowing the structural integrity of my soul and its well-being depended on my oversight. I was the foreman of this construction site for a new life.

I had seen the story I *could* have, and wanted only to defy it. Most importantly, I carefully chose the man with whom I'd continue to build my new home. His gentle hands, soft words, pure heart, and unwavering patience retaught me the very definition of love. In his arms I felt completely at home, and completely at peace. I credit him for seamlessly unraveling bits of the poison web I had not yet shaken free from. Home can be a person. Together we found that the bricks of rebuilding were not as heavy with two sets of hands to carry them.

Keep lifting. Keep building. Update blueprints as needed.

Goodbye is painful, even when necessary. By twenty-four I was engaged to this love of my life and planning our wedding, with both of us on career trajectories that promised us the world ... and all within the city where I'd lived my whole life. The idea of leaving the truest consistency within my definition of home—the very ground beneath my feet, the city I grew up in—had never crossed my mind. Every person I cared for was within arm's length in that town; it was my community. I will always love that city so dearly. And I wouldn't have left, if not for one exceptionally unforgettable night that proved the dysfunction from my past would linger. Sparing you the specifics, I share now only the aftermath. Crying in my fiancé's arms, I said the words that changed our lives: "Get me out of here."

My deep belief is that the universe shows you exactly what you need to see exactly when you need to see it. Divine timing is one of the most painful, yet graceful, themes weaving through my life. I learned to open my eyes, even in the dark, because it is always there.

My husband-to-be had job offers in a handful of states, so we picked one, bought a house, and moved our lives to a place we'd set foot in only once. A decision made in July brought a whole new world in October. Those proved to be the final bricks we needed to build the home we'd been working on. No longer would we allow the remnants of a home demolished long ago to sneak into our building supplies as we attempted to create something new.

It was not easy to leave every familiar street, story, and soul I'd ever known, to have not a single friend within a day's drive. Every room I entered was new, and every face within it clueless to who I was. Starting over meant doing many scary, hard things—alone. Letting go in any form is painful, but *this* release truly changed everything.

Countertops, floorboards, light fixtures, throw pillows. Finishing touches.

I threw away insecurity and fear, having no room for them in my new home. Rather I sought joy, connection, and involvement in this new place. In just eighteen months, I've formed meaningful new friendships, joined gyms, played in a kickball league, gone to local festivals and parades, had a Cinderella moment at a charity ball, and led a chapter of a women's empowerment and networking group. I am finally living in my dream home, the one filled with true peace, happiness, and safety, curated by myself, for myself. I realized only after becoming "happy" what that word actually means. I do not dread opening my eyes in the morning, and do not fear what the day has in store for me.

My process of building a new home evolved over a seven-year journey. Once I abandoned the remains of my original home, home was first a basement. Then, a dog. Eventually, home was a man. It took years for home to actually become a house and a new town. The people and spaces I allowed into my heart built me in return. I am—we all are—a product of our environments, so the commitment to designing each aspect surrounding where I lay my head at night is imperative. I have built this happy home with intention. Let go, condemn, demolish, and rebuild until you're *home*.

Kay Pierson is fiercely passionate about empowering women to embrace their innate worth and potential, and she helps them with genuine connections as a chapter leader for Women Empowering Women, a networking organization. As a devoted wife, she finds fulfillment in the life partnership she's chosen. Her spirituality, independent from traditional religion, serves as a guiding light through all of life's highs and lows. Professionally, Kay commits herself wholeheartedly to her mortgage clients, and finds her work enabling the aspiration for homeownership to be her true calling. The value of a home, and the lives created within it, is dear to her.

Lori Stock

Embrace the Suck

"Embrace the suck." This phrase from military slang means your life is going to suck for a bit but you'll get through it. You've likely heard the more common phrase, "Man plans, and God laughs." I had no idea how true that would be for me in 2018 and 2019. My journey started with what seemed a harmless lump in my neck and ended with a cancer diagnosis, a career-ending autoimmune condition, getting "canned" from my job, and the death of my stepmother. I had a plan, and God said, "Hold my beer and watch this."

Before you light yourself on fire reading that statement, there *are* some funny parts to this drama. If you've never heard or said this phrase, "Mom, I sh*t in your sweatpants," you might be intrigued to learn more. So, let's get to it.

When I made a promise to myself that I wanted to reach a goal weight of 180 by the end of summer 2019, I *really* should have been more specific about how to get there. The chemotherapy and puking program was a bit extreme. And I did *start* with a better plan …

In the summer of 2018, I played golf with a very good friend, and he was in terrible physical condition. For me, seeing him in this shape led to a "don't be that guy" moment. After we—correction: after *I* finished playing golf, I headed straight to a gym to sign up. I began working out, riding bikes, and getting myself in better shape.

After one bike ride, driving home, I discovered a tiny friend had joined my ride on the Katy Trail. As I evicted the tick from its anchor on my neck, I found a large lump I hadn't noticed before. Round, mobile, and nothing to worry about, said the "doctor" (aka me). Doctors really do make the worst patients, as is said, and we don't take care of ourselves like we do our patients. Truth.

Seeing my primary care doctor for a physical soon after, I noted, "Oh, by the way, I have this lump in my neck." She replied, "Huh. Let's get a CT scan just to make sure. It's probably nothing." CT completed, I heard nothing for about ten days and figured no news was good news.

Then, treating patients one afternoon, I was pushing to finish the day because I had Cardinals baseball tickets behind home plate. Treating a patient, I let my doctor's call go to voicemail. But my curiosity got the better of me, and at my first break in the schedule, I listened to the voicemail.

When the doctor says, "You can call me at home to discuss your CT results," the news is never good. I called her and heard my heart beating in my chest along with the words nobody ever wants to hear. "It looks like lymphoma, and it may have metastasized to your spine." Holy *cr*p*!

I continued to treat patients until I could take another break to call my mom. She asked if I was still going to the game. Yep! Seats behind home plate were too good to miss, especially as my life was about to get too complicated for baseball games. Putting this whole thing out of my mind, I enjoyed a Cardinals game with my friends.

I named my node "Bertha," and the next step in her adventure was an abdominal CT with contrast. The morning of the test, I had a stress-induced headache to beat the band. I don't advise slamming back the contrast drink stuff. I managed to get through the test and was on my way home before the outcome of that poor choice landed as a wave of nausea. I pulled over toward the center of the road, and I can affirm that the grassy median on Winghaven Boulevard was thick and well kept … though is maybe no longer quite as tidy at that spot.

I went to my mom's to recover, just in time for the other downside of contrast. I was sick again and also experienced an "SAS" valve failure (acronym for sh*t/air separator). In other words, I pooped in my pants. My mom gave me a pair of her sweatpants to wear just in time for wave number three. Mom came in to check on me, and here's how the conversation went.

Me: "Mom, I sh*t in your sweatpants. I've never said that before."

Mom: "No one has ever said that before."

Now it was time to serve Bertha the node her eviction notice, because 2018 ended with my stepmother's diagnosis of terminal cancer. She lived in Texas, so, knowing I would travel to be with her, I wanted Bertha not to come along. So Bertha and two friends I named Beavis and Butt-Head were removed in February 2019. Those sidekicks bought me a ticket in the stage III club for lymphoma.

Chemotherapy started, with nausea I imagine was a little like what it would be after drinking shots of formaldehyde. Well, maybe the nausea was not as bad as that would have been … who knows. You learn many lessons in humility as you undergo chemotherapy. You lose your hair, and all foods taste like metal or embalming fluid. You say to yourself, *I'm going to eat only healthy things* … then quickly shift that to *whatever stays down*. This is where the suck really started. I had to embrace it because God's plan was clearly for this to happen, and that's the biggest lesson in humility.

During my "classes" to learn humility, I started having a lot of trouble with little tasks like eating, sitting up, walking, and cutting meat. I kept telling the doctors something was wrong. I got the proverbial "There, there." response until one day someone heard me. The oncologist sent me to a "neuro dude," where a blood test revealed a CK (creatine kinase) level of 6000 (normal is between 30 and 300). After the collective "holy cr*ps" from the medical staff, I had an appointment with the neuromuscular clinic at Barnes Hospital.

My good friend Stevie took me to that Friday appointment. Public service announcement: If you face-plant on your way into the neuromuscular clinic, they let you go to the head of the line. They did some tests, and, before I knew it, I was the hit of the clinic. Every resident was in my room; I should have sold tickets. The attending came in and said they were admitting me for the weekend, to add a muscle biopsy on Monday. The conversation went like this.

Doctor: "We're admitting you."

Me: "No, you're not."

Doctor: "How do you take care of yourself?"

Me: "Badly, but I manage. Besides, I have a pet that needs my care, and I can be miserable at home. I've gotten very good at it."

Doctor: "But you need to stay here."

Me: "I'm not staying at this giant petri dish you call a hospital. In fact, my oncologist might have something to say about me being here. I'll see you Monday."

At this point, Stevie's job was to slam me in a wheelchair and make a run for it. They found that the motor control symptoms were due to a condition called necrotizing polymyositis. Hooray! Now we knew what it was so we could treat it. The treatment is one thousand milligrams of prednisone once per week. By the way, if you want to know about LifeLock or the Bissel Pet Pro, I can tell you all about it. With that dosage of prednisone, you don't sleep.

And remember: I was also receiving chemo after the surgery that excised Bertha and her two friends. After my last treatment, I got on the scale and … Congratulations! I reached my goal weight! What a ride, though.

My stepmother passed away only a couple of weeks later, so my ride on the medical roller coaster and the suck-embracing were not over. I was executor of her estate, adding a few more chainsaws to juggle. Thank you, God! But when I stopped and thought more about it, He knew I was ready for this next challenge. In fact, I began to recover from the suck of my illnesses and was able to manage her affairs.

Getting "canned" was the proverbial cherry on top of the year of suck. God knew that was *not* the place to be. He saw to it that I was removed from that sh*t show. My career did not have any anointing, and it was time to put that away.

As I reflect on this chapter of my life, I am filled with gratitude for the lessons learned, the relationships strengthened, and the resilience discovered. While the journey may have been arduous, it has ultimately transformed me into a person of greater empathy, compassion, and purpose.

Lori Stock | Embrace the Suck

Lori Stock is an old mechanic from the Air Force, where she worked on fighters, F-4s, T-38s, and the F-15 Eagle. When she finished her career playing around on airplanes, she decided to become a Doctor of Chiropractic. When you think about it, the leap from airplane mechanic to body mechanic isn't all that long! She was still fixing broken sh*t. Lori lives in O'Fallon, Missouri, with her eighty-four-year-old mother and two cats, Lucy and Ethel. She enjoys many hobbies, including woodworking, reading, swimming, and being charming. Lori employs humor to deal with most situations, believing that life is hard enough without overcomplicating it.

Jessica Beeson

Who Makes the D*mn Rules, Anyway?

Who do you think makes the d*mn rules, anyway?
*What the h*ll do you think you're doing?*
You think you're better than everyone else?
Are you crazy?
Are you stupid?
*You aren't smart enough to figure out how to clean a d*mn table properly. What makes you think you're smart enough to outsmart me?*
You're just a woman.

These are a small sample of the "nicer" insults spoken to me throughout my life. For as long as I can remember until just days before I sat down to write this chapter, phrases like these have followed me through every stage of life (and I am sure they will be there to follow me through the next one). The good news is that, thanks to my peaceful and uncomplicated upbringing, I'll be ready for them. Oh, and by "peaceful and uncomplicated," what I really mean is "chaotic and traumatic." But I'm guessing you knew that was coming.

While there were good moments throughout my childhood, the majority of it was plagued by incredibly painful physical, sexual, and emotional abuse. From the age of five until I was eighteen years old,

I experienced some of the most horrific things imaginable, the scars of which I still bear on both my body and my mind. While my early experiences taught me all about the evils in this world long before I could write about them, they also taught me how to adapt … and how to survive. Through these tough life lessons, I became resourceful, resilient, and strong, even as a child, with survival skills many don't acquire until later in life.

The statistics on childhoods like mine aren't exactly on my side. The 2020 U.S. Census Bureau reported that 40 percent of children who grew up in single-mother households like mine were living in poverty; 63 percent were more likely to be victims of sexual, physical, and emotional abuse; 68 percent were more likely to abuse drugs and alcohol, and 82 percent were more likely to experience increased obstacles in education, career opportunities, and health.

For the longest time I thought all of these "more likely" statements were *rules*—rules that were nonnegotiable. I didn't know who made the rules. Someone did, but that "someone" wasn't me. I didn't get to make any rules, so I must obey *these* rules … right?

I was fourteen years old when I broke my first "nonnegotiable." After I tore my ACL in my right knee and needed a full reconstruction surgery that left two screws in my knee, I was told I would never fight in another kickboxing match or earn my black belt. I was eighteen years old when I broke the second nonnegotiable rule, becoming the first woman in my family to go to college. I rewrote another "rule" when I graduated with my Associate of Arts in Teaching three years later. Then another when I earned my Bachelor of Arts in English Education two years after that.

My entire college experience was a series of me rewriting the "rules." From emancipating myself from my mom so I could attend a four-year university, to spending three full days tracking down the right people to get the required permission to commute the forty-five-minute drive to campus every day rather than live on campus, I broke through every obstacle that popped up its irrelevant and spiteful head.

Each of these obstacles showed up as a "rule," but as General Douglas MacArthur once said, "Rules are mostly made to be broken," and boy do I enjoy breaking them. I had no idea this was just the beginning of a long list of "rules" I would not only break but completely rewrite out of my family history book altogether. Those college years were also the first time in my life when I believed in myself enough to ask what was possibly the most life-altering question I've ever asked myself: "What *else* could be rewritten?"

That core question led to more: What if I *can change* the rules? What if I *am stronger* than they think I am? What if I *am smarter* than they think I am? What if I *already am* all these things? As I thought about these questions, the voices from my past experiences rolled through my head, one after another.

You tore your ACL and had a total reconstruction surgery on your knee. You're never going to fight another kickboxing match, and you'll never become a black belt. A year later, I did both of those things.

You can't go to college because no other woman in your family has and you can't afford it. A year later, I enrolled at my local community college.

You'll never graduate. Five years later, I walked across a stage to receive my second college degree.

The only way to teach is to be in a district and follow all of the district's policies, regardless of the negative consequences on your students. Six months later, I started my own tutoring company.

Women like you with Hashimoto's disease and ovarian cysts will most likely never have children. Enter a red-headed baby girl.

You're just a woman. You don't know anything about business. It's been twelve years in business, and I'm still going strong.

You can't win a Small Business Association award or become an international bestselling author or start a second successful company that allows you to inspire, lift up, and support other women. Oh, wait. I've already done all that too!

And then came the last voice.

You're just a weak little girl. I can do whatever I want to you. I can beat you. I can burn you. I can break you, and there's nothing you're ever going to do about it. You'll never escape from me. Every time you look at the scars on your body, you will remember me. Every time you even think you have a chance to escape, you'll remember who *makes the rules. You'll remember the truth, and you'll remember that I* own *you.* For a long time, I believed every one of these things he told me, until I realized who *actually* made the rules of *my* life: me. I did. Not him. Me.

The moment I realized *I* was the one who had the power to write the rules that dictated *my* life was the moment that *everything* changed. I was ready to make changes. I was ready to fight back. I was ready to reclaim my power. I was ready to rewrite some d*mn rules. I knew this war wasn't one I could win overnight. I knew there would be many battles ahead of me, but I also knew I was finally ready to fight each and every one of them.

Changing rules began with therapy, where I learned to create a supportive environment by surrounding myself with positive influences. Connecting with people who believe in my potential is one of the most vital aspects of my healing. I sought out mentors. Specifically, I found women who had succeeded in their own healing journeys and were willing to share their wisdom. They offered invaluable advice on how to navigate my emotions, conquer my fears, and break free of my past traumas. These women helped me find and create opportunities that I may never have found on my own.

This support network became my foundation, reminding me that I am not alone. It also created a safe space that allowed me to understand my struggles, and encouragement to develop solutions that saved my life. By being intentional about the *people* I spent time with and the *spaces* I put myself into, I found clarity and strength I didn't know I had.

Another rule change was that I took as many steps as I could toward my goals, no matter how small those steps seemed. I wrote down my needs, wants, and dreams … and then I mapped out a plan to achieve them. I listened to podcasts on specific topics, signed up for workshops, trainings, and other courses to propel me forward in both my business and personal aspirations. I stopped watching TV shows with scenes that trigger post-trauma stress responses. I listened to music that was uplifting and inspirational instead of angry and depressing.

All of these rule-changing strategies helped me stay focused, encouraged, and moving forward. With every step, I grew stronger, more resilient, and more confident. I was no longer bound by someone else's rules for my life. I was creating my *own* path, reclaiming my *own* power, and writing my *own* d*mn rules. Therapy helped me heal, and the voices of other women who'd walked similar paths gave me courage. These voices guided me until I could find my own voice and stand, not just as a survivor but as a champion for other women until they, too, are once again strong enough to stand on their own.

Now, instead of living in fear, holding myself back, and listening to rules made by someone else, I take any moment I can to stand in front of the nearest mirror and recite three simple sentences:

Who makes the d*mn rules, anyway?

You do, my beautiful Queen.

You do.

Jessica Beeson | Who Makes the D*mn Rules, Anyway?

Jess Beeson is the founder and CEO of Willow Tree Tutoring LLC and Jess B. LLC. After earning her Bachelor of Arts degree in Middle School English Education from Lindenwood University, she dedicated eight years to the public school system before venturing into entrepreneurship in 2012 with her tutoring company. In 2022, she expanded her entrepreneurial ventures with Jess B. LLC, introducing the transformative "Be You. Be Free." program. Through this program, participants gain valuable insights into the *what*, *why*, and *how* of overcoming obstacles and embracing personal growth. Jess has been married to her husband for nineteen years, and they have a beautiful, smart, and spunky daughter. In her free time, you'll most likely find Jess spending quality time with her family and friends, or dancing and singing like the whole world is watching (and loving every minute of it).

Dr. L. Carol Scott

Childhood Replayed

Standing on the other side of the table, looming over me, with her curled hands knuckles-down halfway across the table, she narrowed her eyes to slits as the ugly words slithered from her lips like a snake's tongue. As her venom filled the small space between us, my default strategy of dissociation kicked in. Cultivated during more than a decade of childhood sexual abuse, this well-developed escape mechanism saved me in my youth and served me well in this moment. My memory is only a silent film, though: full-color video of the scene but no sound.

Though I cannot remember them, I can guess her words because her message by then was repetitive and familiar. Although I was nearly ready for a crucial flash of insight that would finally end her emotional abuse, in *this* moment I simply leapt away. Her verbal poison landed on the table between us as tears streamed from my downturned eyes.

My partner of almost twenty years, our only witness, stepped boldly forward, literally intervening by inserting her arm and leaning her upper body between us. Shouting, "*Stop! Just stop it!*" she broke the tension, allowing awareness to return to my body. I somehow got out of my chair and that room, retreating to safety to continue sobbing.

Looking back from a perspective of almost twenty years, today I can answer the painful question, *How did I not see* this woman and her *destructive behavior for so long?* Beyond knowing her intimately as my dear friend and respected spiritual teacher, what was it that blinded me to her obviously toxic patterns? I cannot deny that for several years I witnessed this behavior directed at others and stayed silent. *Then she turned on me.*

I *so* wish I could tell you that strong self-awareness, healthy boundaries, and well-honed attunement to interpersonal dynamics led me to walk the h*ll away from that "friendship" that very day. But no; not yet. My School of Life required this intensive, upper-division course, which demanded more lessons before my final exam.

No surprise, then, that graduation day began with one final lesson: another episode of cruel words attacking my self-esteem like fangs lunging for an unprotected jugular. My vicious-tongued friend and mentor held prominence and power as cofounder and co-owner of all physical assets for the operation of our nonprofit's programs, roles that ensured her visibility. Inevitably, these verbal attacks *had* been witnessed by others on our team of volunteer staff. To me, it seemed that everyone *always* saw what was happening to me ... but rarely intervened. Yes, just as I had not spoken up for others.

This final instance of verbal violence directed at me also had its witnesses, and after I once again escaped to lick my wounds in the safe space of my living quarters, one of those witnesses followed me to ask, "Are you OK?"

As I stumbled to articulate for her the pain, confusion, and complete inability to understand why my longtime and beloved friend was treating me so, her reply went something like, "Well, some of us have learned not to provoke that kind of reaction in her."

This classic gaslighting defense of a family member engaged in domestic violence simultaneously pierced my mind and heart with a single dagger of truth. My internal *Holy shite!* reaction led me straight to my laptop before the door closed behind her. I entered the term "cycle of domestic violence" into the search engine, seeking to recall these four stages accurately: building tension, an incident of abuse, reconciliation, and calm ... and then back to building tension toward the next abuse. And around we'd go again.

The scream of recognition in my mind escaped my lips as only a low groan of pain and self-disgust. After almost two decades of recovery from incest, I realized I was living as a victim once again.

I possessed enough strength and self-awareness in that moment to call exactly the right friend. Ugly-crying over the landline connection—long before Zoom or FaceTime were born—I spilled my ranting, confused, horrified realizations into her caring ears. Finally exhausting my crazy, fuming, blithering tirade (my version of "hitting bottom," as they say in twelve-Step programs), I heard her gentle offer, "Do you want to hear what I think?"

Knowing I *could* say no, and also familiar with her wisdom, I agreed to hear what came through the phone line next.

"When you were a child, you *couldn't get away*. But now you can."

There it was. Our team, a chosen spiritual family, echoed the dynamics in my birth family! This newly recognized cycle of violence fell comfortably into place, right next to a drama dance familiar from childhood. The awareness that both were pieces in one big puzzle was crystal clear in that instant.

Years before, when I first attended this nonprofit's spiritual development programs as a student/seeker, I had been welcomed as a Golden Child. My skills and talents saluted and nurtured, I was praised volubly and in front of others. Several years later, when the cofounder/owner invited me to join the leadership development program and—two years later—the staff, I saw her as my dear friend and fondest champion.

And she remained so for a few years, as we codeveloped programs and resources for the nonprofit. Never receiving payment for my significant time investment as a staff member, I also gave generously of my resources to support the never-ending financial needs of a small, badly managed nonprofit. Fully "behind the curtain" of the wizard, I was also a board member.

And then something shifted. At first, changes were subtle; I didn't see what was coming. But suddenly my role as the *I Can Do No Wrong Girl* was edited out of our shared story. I began to slip from favor. At first, I heard growing criticism for skills that she previously lauded. Then my talents were no longer required and newer, fresher faces ascended in her favor. Instead of public praise, she criticized me openly in team meetings. Conversations between her and other volunteer staff fell into silence when I entered the room.

Over time, I felt a growing sense of exclusion. I was no longer *in* the leadership circle running the organization, but on the outside, unable to see through heavy curtains. More and more, I discovered decisions long after they were made, heard I'd crossed lines I didn't know existed, or failed to meet expectations never communicated. I felt growing confusion, unable to understand what had gone sideways. Why was I suddenly a problem child, rather than a Star Performer in our little show?

Painful as these changes were, they paled in comparison to the next stage. Soon, this "friend" was reframing my best intentions, distorting the lenses through which other team members viewed me. Manufacturing motivations completely alien to what truly drove my choices, she rewrote the story of my behavior. Other beloved members of our community began to see me differently and behave differently with me, as her whispered interpretations of my actions reshaped their image of me.

In that drop-to-my-knees moment, staring in horror at the image on my laptop screen, a wise voice within led me to a midwife for the birth of my firm resolve: *I am effin* done *with this.* My wise friend who calmly stated the fact "When you were a child, you couldn't get away. But now you can" served as the doula for the newborn who grew into *this* me.

It takes time for a baby to grow to the age of reason at seven years, and decades more to become a fully functioning, integrated adult. The newly birthed, stronger version of Carol needed time to unpack this experience, to see it clearly, and to integrate all the lessons in this School of Life curriculum. After I broke free, I spent long hours discussing my experiences with my former partner, key witness to it all. I journaled, reflected, read, and grew to understand …

This painful dynamic of domestic violence with a friend, mentor, and—I thought—spiritual superior was an enormous mirror reflecting my childhood. My little sibling group, the five of us, were similar in all the essentials to the staff team at this nonprofit. All of us bright, skilled, and talented, and all of us striving to grow and learn from a powerful, damaged adult.

I realized that, like my spiritual mentor, my mom elevated one of us to Golden Child status, always. And that shiny role rotated, changing at her whim. First one of us received her favor, then another, wearing the "can do no wrong" halo. As you may guess, one downside of this role is that it implies the opposite: a Black Sheep, another role that can be reassigned at will.

My decision to leave my chosen spiritual family devastated me. This loss in my early fifties shredded my sense of self and filled me with grief. I left one toxic person but also a home in a community where I thought I would live for decades more.

Now I can see this life passage as "simply" the hardest course I ever took in self-awareness and personal identity. That strangely transformative period of my life fueled the creation of a powerful solution for myself: the Self-Aware Success Strategies, or SASS. This child development–based framework for personal growth lifted me to greater joy, meaning, and authenticity. Now it lifts others too.

Among the seven strategies, my SASS of Independence benefited from a thorough workout in this intensive course. I am now grateful for that education in being my S.E.L.F.—a Self-governed, Ego-aware person, Leading my life, Free of self-imposed barriers. Today my inner sense of worth is mostly unshakable: firm and steady as a concrete slab under my emotional feet. Cruel words no longer collapse me into tears. Rather, they invoke my compassion for the speaker. *Oh, sweetie, who hurt you?*

The enduring BIG PRINT lesson from this passage is so simple it's almost trite. Ready? I *will* repeat the patterns of my childhood and recreate the dynamics of my family until I become self-aware enough to *see* them. I will forever find my perpetrator father, emotionally immature mother, confused and wounded siblings, and my cold and subtly shaming grandparents in other humans. I *will* find avatars for all of them, to continue acting out my little girl roles, fantasies, and fears … until I understand. Until I write myself a new script.

Always, specters from my past stand ready to show up embodied in my friends, colleagues, and acquaintances. In recognition of that reality, I commit to empower myself with emotional growth and continually expanding self-awareness. I commit to getting past my personal drama of a replayed childhood, to allow *y'all* to drop *my* old screenplay. I commit to seeing you as your true self, rather than an echo of my past, and to letting you see me.

Now I live a new story, and, friend, it's some excellent improvisational theater!

From a career focus on how we humans become who we are, Dr. L. Carol Scott launched a mission to develop your SASS—your Self-Aware Success Strategies. She returns you to the surprising power of SASSy social and emotional intelligence from your early years. Concurrent BA degrees in Human Development and Anthropology, an MA in Early Education, and a PhD in Developmental Psychology are the educational foundations for Carol's stellar career. Perhaps most importantly, her forty-year public career paralleled her personal evolution, as she moved through recovery from significant childhood trauma. Today Carol supports others who long to finally "grow up" past their childhood stories and wounds, with her books, keynotes at conferences, and success coaching. Her monthly SASSy Sunday Salon and five-day RISE Virtual Coaching Series offer free samples of how her framework applies to your life.

Cathy Davis

The Bird's the Word

We love our covered front porch. Built circa 1940, it extends across the front of our historic red-brick home on a narrow, tree-lined street in mid-America. Think of the 1950s television show *Father Knows Best* or the 1950s neighborhood scenes in the movie *Back to the Future*. You'll get the picture.

Although our neighborhood is more urban than suburban, we have many critters—raccoons, possums, wild turkeys, red foxes, and even a badger—living behind my neighbor's garage. We also have many big birds: night owls, hawks, egrets, crows, and pigeons who like to nest on our front porch.

The saga started last year when a pigeon couple decided they loved our porch as much as we do—specifically, the porch light immediately next to our front door. They saw it as a great location for their roost (never mind the one on the other side of the porch where they'd have more privacy). Perhaps they are late sleepers, and that side gets too much morning sunlight for pigeons.

The young, cooing couple immediately began their approximately six-month non-approved lease, landing their never-ending bird droppings on the mail table and teaching us that pigeons are the world's messiest birds. These two also must have flunked Aviary Architecture 101, as they constantly replenished the ongoing dissemination of their loosely constructed lean-to. Their "nest" was made from piles of trash—it was never really anything close to what humans (or other birds) would call a nest. They didn't weave intricate basketry ... it was much more like "Let's set a leaf and a piece of straw here, and we'll call it 'home'!" until the spring winds blew it all away and they started over. Another fun fact we learned is that pigeons are continuous-breeding creatures. When you see what you think is the last baby fly from the nest and you get their mess cleaned up, they start rebuilding and are already making more bird babies. After the third round, we found six-inch, steel, bird-deflecting spikes to place on top of both lights, hoping that would deter the flying squatters. The pigeons took heed and found residency elsewhere.

Spring arrived early the following year, and for about one week we basked in the glory of winning the Battle of the Birds with our spikes. Then, in flew the Robin family. Never underestimate the determination of a Mama Robin. This one apparently graduated from the Batman School of Survival.

Catching my eye one morning as she glided in so elegantly, landing atop the tip of a six-inch steel spike, she locked her eyes with mine, then tilted her head as if to say, "Hey, human! You think these shiny spikes scare me? Let me show *you*!" as she proceeded to weave her nest threads among the spikes. This Mama Robin's point of view (POV) regarding the steel spikes differed significantly from the pigeons'. This Mama Robin was apparently the Dean of Aviary Architecture. She used those spikes to her advantage, building her nest "foundation" among them. She then kept building *up above* the spikes, creating a soft bed to roost. There is no way *that* nest would blow away in the gale-force spring winds we have in the Midwest. Very clever, Mama Robin. Quite impressive! There was also no way I was going to evict such an intelligent bird. I wanted to see this play out.

Mama Robin's appearance came at the perfect time to remind me to rethink my own POV on a few things. Was Mama Robin my new Spirit Animal? I've always been fascinated by Spirit Animals and the meaning behind animal appearances in my life. Spirit Animals typically appear in our lives to share a message through their unique nature and skills. Each Spirit Animal has its own methods of overcoming the many daily challenges it meets in order to survive. They do not necessarily guide us but, instead, come to teach us what we need to learn to meet the challenges we are experiencing. Spirit Animals always appear at the right time and place when we are ready to accept them and the wisdom they bring. They remind us to awaken to the synchronicity of life and teach us to be aware of the hidden messages in everyday experiences. We always meet the Spirit Animal whose lesson we most need to learn at precisely the right time.

In my mind, Mama Robin's appearance was no accident. Our business has been experiencing a growth spurt, and as with any new growth, there have been a few hiccups. We have all heard that a Robin is a harbinger of spring, rebirth, and new beginnings. It also symbolizes planting seeds for growth, determination, and good fortune. I was ready to hear Mama Robin's message, and that awareness allowed me to recognize my choices.

Pedal like a Pigeon.

You see, I used to be the pigeon. In years past, every time my business started to grow, I would lift my foot *off* the proverbial gas pedal. My internal Itty-Bitty-Shifty Committee would start singing their song, "Who do you think you are, trying to grow a business?" "You have no clue what you are doing!" Or my favorite, "What makes you think you're smart enough to pull *this* off? You've never done this before."

As a pigeon, I would cave into the siren songs of the Itty-Bitty-Shifty Committee and settle for a half-dressed nest, expecting it to fall apart and blow away. I, too, continued to rebuild—constantly going in circles and crashing at the end of each day in total exhaustion.

Rise like the Robin.

This time is different. I can feel it. I feel the adrenaline pumping with the challenge. I've set new goals for myself and the business. I now choose to …

- Challenge myself to try new things outside my comfort zone.
- Secure my vision in a strong foundation and rise above my doubts.
- Keep an eye on what's happening around me and, to quote Nemo, "Just keep swimming!"

I've gained a lot of respect for Mama Robin. I see the shiny spikes (aka hurdles), and Mama Robin is right! I am following her lead and finding the audacity—and my own weaving style—to *do it anyway*!

Watch me!

Fly High Like a Hawk.

My mother used to talk about finding comfort in seeing a cardinal bird after someone died. She believed that seeing a cardinal was a sign from the one who had passed, telling the living that they were still thinking about us and had stopped by for a visit to let us know they were doing fine.

Mom's nursing home window overlooked a small urban "forest," where she would watch the Cooper Hawks for hours as they flew above the trees, hunting for breakfast. One day, while I was visiting, she declared, "I'm coming back as a hawk!" I asked, "What happened to the cardinal?" She replied, "Hawks fly higher, soar farther, and control the forest."

My mother passed away in the Spring of 2011. While awaiting family to fly in for the funeral, a few of us were sitting on our front porch, watching the world go by. The lawn sprinkler rotated in the front yard, and, sure enough, a Cooper Hawk flew out of the sky and landed in the middle of the lawn, positioning itself for the full advantage of the sprinkler spray. We froze. It watched us, and we watched it as it cooled off in the dancing rotation of the sprinkler, and then it flew away as unexpectedly as it arrived. Coincidence? Maybe. Maybe not.

A few days later, the family was being shuttled from a more formal graveside funeral to a Celebration of Life service at the nursing home. We had arranged the second service to include her friends and caretakers and let them meet the extended family. Sitting in the car at the stoplight, ready to turn into the parking lot, lo and behold … there sat a Cooper Hawk on an old brick porch pillar, watching us. Again, we froze. My daughter whispered, "*Mom*! Do you see her?!"

"Yep. I see her."

Books are in Cathy Davis's DNA and have always played a significant role in her life. She believes we all have a story to tell, and by sharing our stories we can make personal connections and make a difference in the lives of others.

Cathy founded Davis Creative, LLC in January 2004 (celebrating twenty years as they publish this anthology!), adding the Davis Creative Publishing division in 2005. As an industry leader, they have helped publish more than 1,600 aspiring authors throughout the U.S. and several foreign countries, including more than 600 Amazon Bestselling authors.

Cathy is an active member of G.R.I.T. Women's Leadership Community, and PWA (Professional Women's Association). She is a recently retired board member of the local St. Louis, Missouri, chapter of the National Speaker's Association (NSA) and former Co-Dean of the St. Louis Speaker's Academy. Cathy lives in St. Louis with her husband, Jack, and their rescue SnickerDoodle, Chewy (aka Chief Barketing Director).

Made in the USA
Middletown, DE
28 September 2024